# CELLCHURCHSOLUTIONS

## Transforming the Church in North America

### Joel Comiskey

Published By CCS Publishing

**CELLCHURCH**
SOLUTIONS

www.cellchurchsolutions.com

Published by CCS Publishing
23890 Brittlebush Circle
Moreno Valley, CA 92557 USA
1-888-344-CELL

Cover and interior design by Keith Sherrer, idesignetc
Editing by Audrey Dorsch

All Scripture quotations, unless otherwise indicated, are from the Holy Bible, New International Version, Copyright ©1973, 1978, 1984 by International Bible Society. Used by permission.

CCS Publishing is the book-publishing division of Cell Church Solutions, a resource and coaching ministry dedicated to equipping leaders for cell-based ministry.

Find us on the World Wide Web at **www.CellChurchSolutions.com**

---

**Publisher's Cataloging-in-Publication**
*(Provided by Quality Books, Inc.)*

Comiskey, Joel, 1956-
    Cell church solutions : transforming the church in
North America / by Joel Comiskey.
      p. cm.
    Includes bibliographical references and index.
    LCCN 2004097051
    ISBN 0-9755819-0-2

    1. Cell churches--North America.  2. House churches--
North America.  I. Title.

BV601.85.C66 2005        262'.26
                 QBI04-200518

"Dr. Joel Comiskey is the most knowledgeable, best informed, and most persuasive chronicler of the cell church movement. His new book on the cell church in North America is ground-breaking and challenging. The cell church has arrived in America."

— RICHARD PEACE, Ph.D Robert Boyd Munger Professor of Evangelism and Spiritual Formation

---

"In our postmodern, U.S. culture, finding innovative ways to do church is essential. Interestingly, the creative approach Joel Comiskey articulates so effectively has its roots in the first-century church. Here is a book that provides practical answers to the tough questions asked by people with a passion for growing communities of believers all over North America."

— DR. PETER N. NANFELT President, the Christian and Missionary Alliance

---

"In Cell Church Solutions, Joel Comiskey does a terrific job of amassing statistics, not only about cell churches, but about the church in general in North America. He shows how we are falling short of doing the one thing Jesus clearly told us to do—making disciples who can do the work Christ expects his body to do. Joel then gives us profiles of more than forty churches in the United States and Canada that have successfully adapted the cell model for their particular communities, so that we can see that, yes, the cell model really can work here. Finally, Joel pulls everything together and gives very practical teaching on what these successful North American cell-driven churches have in common and how others can adapt the cell model to their own locations. Cell Church Solutions is a must read for anyone who wants to explore the idea of using the cell-based model of the church for his or her community."

— NANCY J. LINDQUIST Joy Equipping Ministries

---

"The American Church must face two important facts today. First, North America is a mission field. Secondly, the Holy Spirit is creating new forms of the church that will be necessary if we are to reach our many cultures with the Good News. This work brings significant help in shaping one of the most effective new structures."

— PAUL E. PIERSON Dean Emeritus, School of Intercultural Studies, Fuller Theological Seminary

# Praise for Cell Church Solutions

"This is one of the most courageous books I have ever read exposing the dysfunctions of the North American church. Joel Comiskey throws a lifeline to church leaders who are struggling to measure up to the "super star" pastor sickness that has invaded the church. Cell Church Solutions will recharge your passion as you wrestle through the essential questions needed to help you navigate the transition to becoming a first-century New Testament church within the complexity and disconnectedness of twenty-first-century North American life."

— DAMIAN WILLIAMS Church Planter, Cross Current Ministries, Washington, DC and Founder, Young Leaders Network

"In Cell Church Solutions Joel Comiskey focuses his passion and expertise for building successful cell-driven churches in North America. A chapter full of case studies provides solutions with a voice and a face by including the e-mail addresses of successful North American models. This chapter alone is worth the price of the book. Solutions are backed up with theology, statistics, personal experiences, and common sense. And prayer is properly put forward as the one essential solution. This book will help you find twenty-first-century solutions for twenty-first-century ministry."

— WILLIAM A. BECKHAM Author and Cell Church Consultant

"Joel reveals how diverse the cell church movement has become over the past fifteen years or so. Cell Church Solutions outlines the obstacles to growth that many cell churches face, and at the same time it brings us back to the core values that, if adhered to, would make the cell church successful anywhere in the world—even the U.S.A."

— BILLY HORNSBY Author and cell church consultant

"Joel Comiskey has outdone himself! Cell Church Solutions explains in practical terms how to make a cell church work in North America, regardless of the cell church structure you prefer. Comiskey avoids debating the nonessentials of cell church (Cho versus G12) and focuses on the basic principles of every healthy cell church. Pastors and leaders who are new to the cell-based philosophy and seasoned veterans alike will find useful solutions for reaching the unchurched and making disciples. I plan to give this book to every cell leader in my church. It will be required reading!"

— DAVID GAINEY, Pastor The Oasis at Rita Ranch, Tucson, Arizona

"Finally, a book that clearly addresses critical issues related to cell churches in the North American context! Joel does a masterful job of examining North American culture and addressing critics who contend that cell church ministry is incompatible with life in North America. Every pastor who is involved in or contemplating a cell church plant should read this book. I'm excited by Joel's vision of beginning cell churches that plant other cell churches."

— BILL MANGHAM Regional Director for the CMA in Latin America

---

"Cell Church Solutions: Transforming the Church in North America should give hope to those seeking to grow the church on North American soil. In defining what the church is and how it can function in the North American culture, the author gives basic principles and practices and many case studies that point the way to kingdom effectiveness."

— MIKEL NEUMANN, DMISS Associate Professor of Missiology, Western Seminary International Resource Consultant, CBInternational author and conference speaker on small-group ministries

---

"I am the pastor of a small church that is in transition from a traditional, program-based ministry to a cell-based ministry. Joel's book has hit the nail squarely on the head. For those of us who are struggling in North America to lead our churches to the next level, Cell Church Solutions is a breath of fresh, revitalizing air that not only sweeps away the staleness of old and ineffective ministry models but also captures the mighty wind of the Holy Spirit that is transforming a new generation!"

— BOB MANAGBANAG Pastor, Light and Life Christian Fellowship, Sylmar, California

---

"In Cell Church Solutions, Joel Comiskey has addressed the questions that most North American pastors have been asking about the applicability of cell church to their setting. One by one, he removes the excuses North American pastors have used for not experiencing the dynamic growth of disciples that is seen in the minority world. His explanation of what a cell church might look like in North America gives a picture of possibility and flexibility while not settling for just another way to say "small groups." His practical discussion of the training track will improve the way most churches develop leaders."

— DR. RICH BROWN Dean, Simpson Graduate School of Ministry, Redding, CA

# Praise for Cell Church Solutions

"I have had the privilege of knowing Joel Comiskey for more than twenty-five years as we graduated together in 1982 (that was when he had no children but lots of black hair), and I have followed his amazing, God-blessed ministry with keen interest. This book is a must read for all pastors, small group leaders, Sunday school teachers, laypeople, and anyone else who truly wants to grow their church and the body of Christ. This will be another book that will surely stir the body of Christ."

— DAN CALLAWAY Missions motivator and broadcaster with SEND International

---

"Read this book with a yellow highlighter! Pinch the corners of pages that have important facts! This is not a book to be read but to be used as a guideline. The cell church in America is marching on. This book is the drumbeat for the parade."

— DR. RALPH NEIGHBOUR Author, professor, and church planter

---

"Dr. Joel Comiskey is one of my favorite people. His extraordinary writings grip you, instruct you, excite you, and ignite you about doing cells in your church in the most practical and proven fashion. Do not ignore the powerful instructions in this book! Joel's outstanding research and the inspiring stories makes this a must read book for every Christian leader. No one will put the book down uninspired, and it makes cell groups an adventure. I highly recommend it."

— DALJIT S. GILL Associate Minister, CityLife Church, Melbourne, Australia

---

"I believe that the church method of the future will be home Bible cells. A church can get ready to use cells by reading Cell Church Solutions."

— DR. ELMER L. TOWNS Vice President, Liberty University, Dean, School of Religion, Lynchburg, Virginia

---

"This book is the most relevant material for understanding the practical application of cell church principles into the North American postmodern culture. It provides examples of real, successful cell churches and encourages the church planter to lead the initiation of his church into a more relevant and effective church for twenty-first-century North America."

— RAUL, A. HERNANDEZ Church Planting Missionary in metro Washington DC for the SBC

"My heart flooded with excitement as I read Cell Church Solutions. What a blessing it is to have this balanced, instructive, motivational, and God-inspired book on cell church. This book is for any pastor or leader who wants to make a major impact on its community. Thanks, Joel. You are a gift to the body of Christ!"

— FRANK SEIXAS Founder And Senior Pastor, Oshawa Community Church, Oshawa, Ontario, Canada

"Joel gives practical insights from his observations of cell ministry. The reader has an opportunity to see cell ministry from many vantage points. There are solutions for every challenge in growing healthy cells."

— BILLY JOE DAUGHERTY Senior Pastor, Victory Christian Center, Tulsa, Oklahoma

"Can the Cell Church really work in North America? Cell Church Solutions goes a long way toward forever laying that question to rest by answering with a vibrant and documented, "Yes!" Joel Comiskey documents forty-four growing North American churches, each one cell based or in transition to cell. How are they doing it? Each has gone back to the basics with prayer. They are creating life-giving communities. Through these communities they are reaching out in evangelism and discipling those won to Christ. They are dedicated to developing a cell coaching system to care for their leaders. Not content with simply growth, they see the planting of new cell churches as a key part of their cell DNA. Is this possible for your church? Cell Church Solutions provides needed insight into how you, too, can accomplish this in the midst of our North American culture. Joel has written a must read for those serious about understanding and participating in the North American cell church movement."

— DR. LES BRICKMAN Cell Church Professor/Consultant, NCD Coach, TLC Coach Trainer, and founder of Strategic Cell Ministries International

"Of all Joel's books, Cell Church Solutions provides church leaders with probably the best overall picture of how a cell-driven church is developed and implemented."

— STEVE MACK Lead Pastor, Berlin International Church, Berlin, Germany

# Praise for Cell Church Solutions

"I've read everything Joel Comiskey has ever written! The reason is that he's so practical! I'm not all that interested in debating a bunch of theory or droning on about a bunch of stuff that sounds good on paper but when you really find out about it, things are different. I'm a pastor in the trenches—and Joel provides answers. Joel is great at discovering the real questions pastors and church leaders are asking—and then providing practical helps. His latest book, Cell Church Solutions won't disappoint you. Chapter 5 alone is worth the price of the book—listing church after church, all different sizes and denominations, that are making the cell church model work in North America. Listed are not only information about the church, but loads of web site contacts for further investigation.

But this book goes further, giving helpful insight after insight of the real issues that need to be worked through with your people in order to make a cell church work—not theory, but bottom-shelf basics thoroughly thought through. His emphasis on "The Radical Middle" makes clear it's not about theory, but rather, making this work in your local church. Don't miss buying and reading this book from cover to cover."

— JAY FIREBAUGH Senior Pastor of Clearpoint, Houston, Texas

---

"In tracking the development of the cell movement over the past few decades, Comiskey helps the reader see the dynamic power that cells offer in assisting the Church to become truly a kingdom-oriented movement again. He is comprehensive in raising the technology of this phenomenon thereby keeping our eyes on the true mission of the Church. By Joel's clearly identifying the obstacles that face the North American church and demonstrating how cell solutions address them, for the good of the mission, the reader is compelled to consider the values and vision of becoming a cell/celebration church."

— DR. KEVIN MANNOIA Graduate Chaplain, Azusa Pacific University

---

"Thank you, Joel Comiskey, for writing this long-needed book; it's a valuable resource that will bring encouragement, insight, and guidance to all who want to see the cell church work in North America."

— REV. DR. STEVE CORDLE Senior Pastor, Crossroads United Methodist Church

"Dr Joel Comiskey's insight into the North American Church is phenomenal. He shows the postmodern generation how to serve and shows us how to stay out of our church box and get into an effective cell group ministry that works. Cell Group Solutions is not another lollipop solution for our bookshelf. Comiskey helps us understand secular western culture by showing us how cell ministry actually works in North America."

— DR. ROBERT T. LINN Associate Pastor of Outreach, CrossPoint Community Church, Tucson, Arizona

"Joel simplifies some of the complexities of the cell church; he reduces it to its irreducible essence. A must read for those thinking of doing cell church in North America. Thanks for the help, Joel."

— ROB REIMER Pastor of South Shore Community Church, Bridgewater, Massachusetts

"The author, with his research, draws from the rich experience of cell ministries across the globe and with keen insight makes the necessary cultural adaptations that will make cell ministry effective in the North American church."

— DALE GALLOWAY The Beeson International Center, Wilmore, Kentucky

"Joel Comiskey has established himself as a well-informed consultant in the area of cell based churches. Anything he has to say on the subject is important."

— JAMES M. GRANT, Ph.D. President, Simpson University

"Joel's book is required reading for pastors and leaders of U.S. home group churches."

— DR. JOHN N. VAUGHAN Church Growth Today, Research & Consulting

# Praise for Cell Church Solutions

" Joel Comiskey is a cell church practitioner. His extensive international experience with the cell church, the planting of a cell church in southern California, and his personal coaching pursuits within the North American cell church movement sets him apart from being merely a cell church theorist. In this book, Joel writes about the Radical Middle. An adherent of the Radical Middle desires to make disciples, raise up leaders, evangelize more effectively, and eventually plant new cell churches. Simply put the Radical Middle longs for purity and practicality in the North American cell church. Further, the Radical Middle is all about balance between cell quality and cultural relevance. No book like this on the North American cell church has ever been written. Learn from a humble and prominent voice of the worldwide cell church movement about what God is doing through North American cell churches."

— ROB CAMPBELL Pastor/founder of Cypress Creek Church, Wimberley, Texas

"By contextualizing proven principles from successful cell churches around the world, Joel Comiskey has given North American church leaders a valuable step-by-step manual. I truly believe cell based ministry is the most doable and effective model to position any church for continuous healthy expansion. I am grateful to be under Joel's coaching during our own church's transition to cell based ministry."

— DR. PATRICK CHOW Senior Pastor, Agape Chinese Alliance Church, San Diego, California

"I love this book. It will help North American church leaders determine a direction for their congregations. The book is helpful, factual, practical, and easy to read. It gives leaders an overview and road map on what's working and why. The book allows flexibility from some of the existing models, but also shows that leaders need a systemic plan for long term success. I like the idea that not every church is destined to become a mega church—this fact will liberate many from feelings of failure and will help them determine what God wants them to be."

— DWIGHT DENYES Executive Pastor, Emmanuel Christian Center, Minneapolis, Minnesota

# Table of Contents

# Table of Contents

# Table of Contents

# Foreword

**have been waiting for this book for a long time.** I know of no other one like it. This book holds major keys for us to prepare for a coming move of God in North America. We desperately need revival, and we must begin now to prepare.

We live in exciting days in the history of the church. I believe we are on the verge of a great end-time harvest. Just as God magnetically drew the animals to Noah's ark, He is drawing multitudes of people to Himself in these last days. I meet them week after week as I travel throughout the nations. Statistics show us that the number of people being saved today compared to twenty years ago is escalating. Clearly, the wind of the Holy Spirit is sweeping our world in an unprecedented manner. But I have often grieved when I return to America. What will it take for North America to experience another move of God like we see in many other nations? Much of the answer is contained in this book. The tide is changing! America is beginning to prepare for revival.

During the next few years, as we race toward the last chapter in history, we have a mandate to prepare for hundreds of thousands of souls coming into the kingdom of God in our communities. A great harvest is promised, and it is sure to come (Acts 2:17–18). We must continue to prepare and be ready to care for the harvest when it pours in.

I grew up on a farm. I know that various crops are ready to be harvested at different times of the year. We had to be alert, with our barns and equipment ready, so we could harvest our crops when they were ready. Jesus tells us to be constantly alert and ready. "Do you not say, 'Four months more and then the harvest'? I tell you, open your eyes and look at the fields! They are ripe for harvest" (John 4:35).

Through the ages, the Lord has continually drawn people to Himself. Sometimes, however, a large portion of the harvest was lost because Christians were not alert and ready.

One such huge harvest for which the church in America was not prepared occurred from the late 1960s to mid-1970s. It was called the "Jesus People Movement." This movement began when a number of believers in Christ entered the hippie counterculture and shared the gospel of Jesus Christ, resulting in a massive number of conversions to Christianity among young people. By early 1971, there were Jesus People coffeehouses, communes, and other types of establishments in every state and province across the United States and Canada.

But much of the church was unprepared for this radical new breed of Christians. The tension between the Jesus People and the established churches was a source of irritation for the Jesus People, who saw the church as slow-moving and steeped in tradition and legalism. The church often could not understand these kids with long hair and sandals. Although some churches and Christian communities did welcome these new converts with open arms and disciple them, many new believers fell by the wayside and were disillusioned.

Let's not make the same mistake again! People need more than good sermons to grow; they need a relationship with God and with other Christians with a vision to reach their world. The wineskins for this to be accomplished are healthy cell groups. Early this year I was in Manaus, Brazil, where a few months earlier they had baptized ten thousand new believers in one day! But they had the cell groups prepared to disciple these new believers. Could it be that in North America the Lord is waiting for us to prepare the new wineskins—new cell groups in our churches—for the coming move of God?

Cell Church Solutions is not about another cell church method. It is filled with examples of dozens of healthy cell churches in America that are preparing now for the coming harvest. Joel has done his homework well. Only the Holy Spirit can build the church, and this book gives us tools and biblical insights the Holy Spirit can use in our churches to prepare our towns and cities for the coming revival.

— **LARRY KREIDER,** DOVE Christian Fellowship International

# Introduction

**C**ell-based churches are flourishing overseas. Ever since David Cho and the Yoido Full Gospel Church started the modern cell church movement in the early 1970s, pastors have been fascinated with cell ministry. Then in the 1990s reports surfaced about the explosive growth of César Castellanos's church in Bogota, Colombia, and how this church adapted the cell model to make it work even better.

But what about the cell church in North America? Many pastors and leaders have tried to implement what they discovered from cell churches overseas, but little information exists on the success rate and the cultural adjustments necessary to make it work in North America.

I'm using North America to refer specifically to the United States and Canada. I realize that an official definition of North America includes Mexico. The language and cultural differences of Mexico, however, place it outside the boundaries of this book.[1] Since there are close to 300 million people living in the United States, compared to approximately thirty-five million in Canada, most of the illustrations in this book will be directed to the U.S.

Although I'm focusing on North America, my hope is that the fruit of this study will be applied in other western contexts such as Europe and Australia.

## Lack of information

Most of the cell church literature today is derived from majority world contexts (majority world meaning overseas or third world). My books *Groups of Twelve*[2] and *Passion and Persistence* describe two of the largest churches in Latin America and derive principles from these churches for others to follow. Other books also explore the incredible growth of overseas cell churches.[3*]

---

\* I write extensively about these worldwide cell churches at
www.cellchurchsolutions.com/articles/worldwide/tenLargest.htm

While North American churches marvel at the incredible growth overseas, the immediate question is, Will the same thing work here? North America is simply a different animal, and those ministering in North America understand the unique cultural differences.

Gary Penny, a cell church pastor, echoes the thoughts of many North American leaders by saying, "The cell model traces its lineage back to Cho's church in Korea. How much of the effectiveness of the model is attributed to the Korean culture and how much is actually transferable between cultures?"[4] This book attempts to answer that question.

## Different questions for North America

North American leaders aren't even asking the same questions as their overseas counterparts. The western, post-Christian reality is so different, and the needs so distinct, that the questions are different.

Questions for overseas churches include, How can we reap the harvest? What model will do a better job of managing the growth? What care structure will work best to disciple the multitudes (G12, 5x5,[5] etc.)?

Questions for those living in North America include, How do I get someone to come to my cell group? How do I find people willing to enter the training track and become a future cell leader? How do I motivate my people to submit to their leaders? How can I promote the cell vision?

Pastors and leaders in North America are *not* ignorant of the overseas models; rather, most haven't arrived at the place where a model applies. I've written about the G12 model developed at the International Charismatic Mission (ICM) in Bogota, Colombia. Though many North American pastors are fascinated by ICM's growth, the idea of a cell leader multiplying his or her cell twelve times is so far off the radar screen that it remains in the realm of theory rather than practice for the vast majority of North American churches.

## Missionaries to North America

Every time I visit countries such as Korea, Brazil, Africa, Asia, or Latin America, I go away encouraged and amazed at the health and vibrancy of the church. The so-called *mission field* revives my spirit because of the amazing work God is doing.

The atmosphere in North America, on the other hand, has become increasingly skeptical and post-Christian. It's a harder mission field than many of the overseas locations where the huge cell churches are found. This book is an attempt to understand secular, western culture and then to build a cell strategy based on that difference.

This book is not simply a theoretical exercise. After serving in Ecuador for eleven years, we as a family felt called to leave the "mission field" in South America to minister in North America, our new mission field. In Ecuador we were cofounders of a church that grew to 279 cell groups with 1300 worshippers. The revival atmosphere was exciting as not only our church but many churches were growing. Since returning to North America in June 2001, we've had to adjust to another, more difficult, reality. People aren't running to accept Jesus and become disciples. The ground is harder and the people more secular.

For the past three and a half years we've been coaching pastors who are in transition to cell-based ministry in the United States. We are also planting a cell church in Moreno Valley, California. We started in our home in September 2003 and have continued to multiply cell groups from the first pilot group.[6]

Those ministering in North America and in the western world face unique cultural challenges that need to be understood. Will McRaney, a North American church-growth leader, says, "The challenge before the church and the individual Christian is to exegete not only our message, but also our culture to ensure that our traditions do not hinder our understanding and communication of our message."[7]

Those who implement the principles in this book will have to work hard. There simply is no magical cure. Yet the cell church, better than any other strategy, provides a built-in health mechanism as churches reach out to those without Christ.

## Cell church defined

Cell church in its simplest form is a strategic approach that emphasizes both cell and celebration on an equal basis.

In the cell church, cell is the church and celebration is the church. Every worshipper is encouraged to attend both the weekly cell group and the weekly celebration service.

Most people know what the Sunday church celebration looks like. Worshippers gather to hear the Word preached, worship the living God, and participate in the sacraments (e.g., the Lord 's Supper and baptism).

But what about the cell? The most common definition of a cell (and the one followed in this book) is this: *a group of three to fifteen people who meet weekly outside the church building for the purpose of evangelism, community, and discipleship with the goal of multiplication.*

Implicit in this definition is the overarching goal of glorifying God and achieving spiritual growth in Christ.

All small groups are not cell groups. One of the major differences between cell groups and generic small groups is the cell's emphasis on evangelism, leadership development, and multiplication in each cell.

Cell churches also have other types of ministries (e.g., ushering, worship, prayer, missions, and training). These ministries, however, are not called *cell groups*, even though the particular ministry might be small and a group.

The ministries in a cell church, rather, support the cell and celebration. Everyone participating in a church ministry is also actively involved in a cell group, if not leading one (this is especially true of elder and board leadership).

In the cell church, the cell group is the backbone, or center, of church ministry. Cell ministry replaces the need for many traditional programs.

I like to use the phrase "the cell-driven church" because church-growth success is primarily measured through infrastructure growth as the church grows from the core to the crowd.

Some churches have cell groups as one of the programs in the church. In this scenario, the senior pastor, while overseeing all the programs, delegates the small-group ministry to another person. In the cell church, however, the senior pastor is personally involved in cell ministry and is considered the point person and cell visionary.

## People who should read this book

I'm writing to pastors, church planters, and laypeople who are interested in cell-based ministry.

### Pastors

At one seminar, a participant grilled me about my motivation for writing about cell church. He wanted to know if it was money, fame, or some other motivation that was driving me. I answered, "It's for the little guy."

I'm vitally interested in reaching pastors who struggle with not having enough charisma to emulate the large-church pastors. Many pastors are frustrated because they can't be like _____ (you can fill in the blank).

It's my conviction that most church-growth strategies that rely on attracting a crowd are like pulling a cart up a hill. They are burdensome, and they require that the pastor become a talented entrepreneur, even though most pastors lack the necessary personality and gifting to do so.

Sunday mega models work well for super-talented pastors. But for the common leader who lacks such skills, discouragement is a natural consequence. My passion is to help the pastor who can't attract great crowds but is committed to discipleship and to converting church attendees into lay harvest workers.

I can envision a potential pastor in seminary reading this book and being encouraged to try the cell church strategy. I believe this book will give such a person a viable option for making disciples who make disciples, while growing a healthy church as a result.

### Church planters

When I first planted a church in 1983, I started by renting a house and inviting people to join me in downtown Long Beach, California. Those initial days were filled with delight and excitement. I even taught from David Cho's book, *Successful Home Cell Groups*, and started four cells.

I lacked information, however, on the cell infrastructure, and when we started Sunday morning service, I gave myself wholeheartedly to making sure the attendees came back each Sunday. I became Sunday driven rather than cell driven. I lost the small-group focus, partly because the vast majority of church growth literature at that time focused on how to grow a Sunday morning service. My own denomination, for example, required only a report on Sunday attendance, finances, and membership—nothing on small-group involvement.

The church I founded in downtown Long Beach continues to this day, but it's my conviction that a solid, cell-based vision would have caused this church to soar to greater heights.

My hope is that this book will give confidence and wisdom to start New Testament cell churches throughout North America. With three times as many North American churches closing each year as opening, God desires church planters to answer the call to start new churches. It doesn't take a lot of money or complexity to start a cell church. A church planter can open his or her home, invite people, build a core, multiply the cell, eventually grow to a weekly celebration and continue the process of starting more churches. This book will help the U.S. church planter properly discern the North American context and provide tools to start cell-based ministry.

## *Laypeople*

Since the first section lays out why small groups are so effective, laypeople will be encouraged to press on with small-group ministry and not be discouraged by the many obstacles. In the second section, laypeople will find practical tools to make cell groups work in North America. They will be helped by learning how to pray, how to build small-group community, how to practice group evangelism, and how to exercise the gifts of the Spirit in the cell context. For lay leaders who are coaching other cell leaders, I've dedicated an entire chapter on how to coach more effectively.

---

## Cell Church Solutions

The ministry I started in 2002 is called Cell Church Solutions (CCS). The aim of this ministry is to offer practical assistance to people planting cell churches or attempting to make the transition to cell church in North America and other parts of the world.

This book shares the same name as the ministry because the goal is the same: *to provide help for those doing cell church ministry*. I've purposely linked this book with **www.CellChurchSolutions.com** to provide ample resources for those looking for solutions to implement cell church ministry. Each chapter is filled with practical how-to examples and information so pastors and leaders can actually make it happen.

Throughout this book, I refer to topics on which I have written other books and articles. The articles are available free of charge on the Cell Church Solutions web site. The books can also be purchased on the web site. For a list of available materials, see the Appendix on page 155.

## Two main sections

The first section of this book relates North American culture and church life to cell church ministry.

The second section highlights the unique principles that should be emphasized for cell ministry to work effectively in North America. I chose specific cell principles in this section because they relate to the needs and culture in North America. These principles will help pastors and leaders to make cell church work in the North American context.

# Section **One**

## How the Cell Church fits into North America

## Chapter One

# The State of the North American Church

**A**s I talked with my friend Don Otis about promoting this book in North America, our conversation quickly turned to the state of the North American church. We both started talking about recent research that points to a troubled North American church bombarded with materialism, secularism, and immorality. It wasn't long before the name of George Barna, the leading researcher on the North American church, entered our conversation. Don said, "As I read Barna, I get the impression that he's very discouraged."[1]

"Those are my thoughts exactly," I responded.

Barna, more than any other person, has diligently uncovered what is happening in the North American church scene through hard, factual research. This chapter combines Barna's research, the research of others, and my own personal observations to paint a clearer picture of the North American church.

## Not in Kansas anymore

When we think of the mission field, we often hear exotic names like Timbuktu or Borneo. For too long we've considered going "over there" to do missions. It's now time to realize that the mission field is North America.

North America has so many unchurched people that it's now one of the mission targets of Christians who live in other countries. North American culture, in fact, could be more accurately described as "pre-Christian." Leonard Sweet, professor at Drew University, says, "Only two countries have more nonbelievers than the US: India and China. The US is the third largest mission field in the world."[2]

The general North American population has increased by 15% since 1991. Yet in that same period, the number of people who do not attend church has increased by 92%—from 39 million to 75 million.[3]

It's humbling, yet true, that the North American church is no longer the center of Christianity, as it once was. Bill Easum, respected church consultant, says, "Maybe we're more blessed with bigger incomes, but by every other standard most Christians around the world outshine us."[4]

When I travel and speak overseas, I often receive more encouragement than I give. I come back filled with hope because of the spiritual power and vitality that I see and experience. When the plane lands in North America, however, I realize that I will face another, harsher reality. I describe it as a *lack of forward momentum*. The church seems stalled in its tracks.

The North American church desperately needs another great awakening to keep it from sliding into the same obscurity that the church in Europe is already experiencing.

## Population explosion—church implosion

Often we define church growth by whether a few congregations are growing, rather than looking at the overall church in the nation. It's easy to point to certain mega churches and imagine that North America is exploding with church growth. Statistics, however, point to another reality.

The reality is that there is an overall decline of church growth in North America—even though some mega churches are exploding. Tom Clegg and Warren Bird, in their excellent book *Lost in America*, say, "The explosion of megachurches and other fast-growing congregations has masked the impact of an overall discouraging and negative trend: In the past fifty years, U.S. churches have failed to gain an additional 2 percent of the American population."[5]

The western world is the only major segment of the world in which Christianity is not growing.[6] Church attendance in North America continues to drop, going from 60% after World War II to 49% in 1991 and just over 40% today—although some experts say that Americans are over-reporting their church attendance and the real number is closer to 24%.[7] Whether people are overstating their church attendance or not, we know that there has been a steady decline in attendance and membership in the past sixty years.

Though church attendance is declining, the proportion of those who say they have no religion rose from 9% to nearly 14% between 1993 and 2002. During that same period, the proportion of those who said they belonged to other religions—including Islam—increased from 3% to 7%.[8] Members of non-Christian world religions don't live "over there" anymore; Muslims, Buddhists, and Sikhs live and work along side Protestants and Catholics here in North America.

Much has been written about the proliferation of mega churches in North America.[9] Though we should rejoice in church growth, the reality is that much of the mega church growth is transfer growth—which suits the consumer-shopping mentality of an entrepreneurial society. The fact that some churches are growing rapidly while attendance as a whole is declining should cause us to wonder whether the mega church phenomenon is working. The facts indicate that

- 81% of U.S. churches are either plateaued or declining in attendance
- 18% of U.S. churches are growing primarily by transfer growth
- 1% of the churches are growing by conversion growth[10]

Eddie Gibbs, professor at Fuller Seminary, writes, "Measuring results in terms of increased attendance at worship services and other church-related activities creates a premature sense of achievement. . . . Is one church winning people simply at the expense of other congregations that do not have the resources to compete on equal terms in the religious marketplace?"[11]

---

*In America, it takes the combined efforts of eighty-five Christians working over an entire year to produce one convert. At that rate, a huge percentage of people will never have the opportunity, even once, to hear the gospel....*

---

Conversion growth is just not occurring much in the U.S. Roughly half of all churches do not add one new person through conversion growth.[12] Clegg and Bird write, "In America, it takes the combined efforts of eighty-five Christians working over an entire year to produce one convert. At that rate, a huge percentage of people will never have the opportunity, even once, to hear the gospel in a way they can understand it from a friend they trust."[13]

This book doesn't claim that the cell church offers a quick fix. I do believe, however, that it offers the best solution for sustained growth in both quality and quantity. As chapters three and five demonstrate, the cell church approach makes it possible for all believers to be involved together in reaping the harvest.

## Beyond church attendance

My wife was sharing with one lady who said, "If I go to church, I want a big church where I can sit in the back and no one knows me." My wife invited her to our cell group in Moreno Valley. The lady said, "No, I don't do small churches. Sorry. I just like the big, impersonal ones."

Someone has said that the ABCs of the North American church are *Attendance, Buildings,* and *Cash*—a sad indictment of a church that has lost its way. Larry Crabb, author and psychologist, says, "The future of the church depends on whether it develops true community. We can get by for a while on size, skilled communication, and programs to meet every need, but unless we sense that we belong to each other, with masks off, the vibrant church of today will become the powerless church of tomorrow."[14]

---

*What saddens my heart is that various "model" churches seem to grow through high performance techniques, shorter sermons, and less worship. I call this "Christianity light" to attract non-Christians.*

---

One typical U.S. church that I've worked with experienced rapid growth when Pastor John came to the church in 1989 and focused his church on attracting a crowd on Sunday morning. Between 1989 and 1993, Sunday attendance climbed from 200 to 500. The pastor, however, never prioritized disciple making—even among the staff members. The staff and church geared up all week for the Sunday crowd. In 2001, when the pastor left, the crowd had already shrunk back to about 200.

Gibbs wisely says, "To the extent that worship degenerates into spectatorism, boredom will eventually set in. The seeker-sensitive model requires a continuous flow of creativity in order for the entertainment factor to be sustained. Smaller, resource-strapped churches soon run out of ideas and their performance level is often embarrassingly amateurish and lacking in audience appeal."[15] Audiences tend to drift to the next show in town. In the situation mentioned above, what seemed like great church growth (500 people attending the Sunday service) disappeared when a better church service in town siphoned off the apparent growth (back down to 200).

## Frequent church closures

When my own denomination meets for its annual council gathering, the positive reports of new church plants and spectacular growth are touted, and the failures are quietly ignored. This is human nature and part of the way we act and think. The fact is, however, that three times as many churches in America are closing (approx. 3750 per year) as are opening (approx. 1350 per year).[16]

Church planting is necessary for the church to stay relevant in the twenty-first century. In this book I've dedicated an entire chapter to cell church planting because I believe it's vital. We need pioneers who are skilled at friendship evangelism, prayer, and leading a cell group. Cell ministry is the perfect breeding ground to prepare new pastors and ministers.

## Fog in the pulpit

Satan knows that infecting the church with a deadly virus won't happen with one injection. The virus is introduced gradually through unbiblical preaching. Liberal teaching sprinkled with half truths confuses the hearers, causing them to stray from God's path.

Surveys indicate that 50% of the pastors in the pulpit today *don't* have a biblical worldview.[17] That is, only 50% of the pastors in North America are committed to the accuracy of biblical teaching, the sinless nature of Jesus, the literal existence of Satan, the omnipotence and omniscience of God, salvation by grace alone, and the personal responsibility to evangelize.[18]

The Christian divorce rate continues to spiral out of control—even atheists are less likely to become divorced. The next generation will reap the dysfunctional results, since the next generation is the product of broken families.[19]

What saddens my heart is that various "model" churches seem to grow through high performance techniques, shorter sermons, and less worship. I call this "Christianity light" to attract non-Christians. One pastor near where I live joined the bandwagon to get non-Christians into church by advertising that for one month the theme of his preaching would be the rock group The Beatles. I didn't ask how he planned to make this the theme of his sermons.

Barna wisely says, "The church is fighting a losing battle by trying to become more comfortable and more attractive to the world around them. . . . Church events cannot effectively compete with what the world has to offer. The only thing the Church can provide that no one else has is a life-changing, practical encounter—and on-going relationship—with the living God and with people transformed by similar encounters."[20]

## Materialism

The economy in North America is the envy of the rest of the world. Financial prosperity, mixed with the lure of easy credit card payments, has allowed people to spend more money on a wide variety of adult toys. American advertisers excel in convincing people of their need to buy the latest gadget.

---

*Church strategies, whether cell church or any other strategy,*
*can't change a person's propensity for materialistic greed.*
*Only God can.*

---

Many churches, often unwittingly, have succumbed to the god of personal pleasure and affluence. Twenty-five years ago Dr. Francis Schaeffer warned of the danger that the Church would eventually adopt the two "terrible values" of "personal peace and affluence."

Schaeffer's warning has regrettably become the reality in the North American church. In spite of incredible prosperity in North America, only one out of ten born-again believers actually tithe, and statistics indicate that the more money a person earns, the less he or she is willing to give to the Lord.

It's my conviction that only prayer, fasting, and repentance will overcome this malady. Church strategies, whether cell church or any other strategy, can't change a person's propensity for materialistic greed. Only God can. I believe that God Himself gave us the remedy for change in 2 Chronicles 7:14: "If my people, who are called by my name, will humble themselves and pray and seek my face and turn from their wicked ways, then will I hear from heaven and will forgive their sin and will heal their land."

All of us in North America need to humble ourselves before God, crying out to him for mercy, healing, and revival. The church can't go forward on its feet until it learns to go forward on its knees. The only way that Christianity can truly make an impact in North America is through the power of God manifested through the fervent prayers of His people.

## Hopeful signs

### Small-group involvement

More and more people throughout North America are taking the time to join a life-giving small group. Participation in small groups that focused on prayer, Bible study, and fellowship shot up from 11% in 1994 to 26% in 2004. There seems to be a new excitement in small-group ministry—especially in the western part of the U.S. where small-group involvement jumped 136% in the past ten years.

Other church-oriented activities, however, didn't grow at all. Barna even says, "The findings might indicate that we are entering a new era of spiritual experience—one that is more tribal or individualized than congregational in nature."[21]

People are wanting to experience their Christianity, like they do everything else. Increasingly, people are unwilling to sit while the preacher performs. The pulpiteer who can attract great multitudes is becoming less and less relevant in an age of decentralization, quick movement, and rapid deployment. Perhaps we should take more of our lessons from the church in China, which is rapidly spreading in the homes of members.

---

### Worldwide church explosion

Jesus is Lord of His church, and God is doing amazing things in Africa, Asia, and Latin America. Dr. Philip Jenkins, distinguished professor of history and religious studies at Penn State University, says that in just twenty years, two-thirds of all Christians will live in Africa, Latin America, or Asia.[22] We in the west need to rejoice in this fact, while humbly admitting that the center of gravity for church growth has shifted from the western church to the non-western world.

---

## Mission effort in America

We're on a mission field, and this should refocus all of us ministering in this land. We need missionaries right here, right now. God is looking for church planters and pastors who are willing to study North America the way missionaries study a foreign culture. When Jesus saw multitudes swarming around him, he said to his disciples, "Do you not say, 'Four months more and then the harvest'? I tell you, open your eyes and look at the fields! They are ripe for harvest" (John 4:35). Christ's strategy was always to make disciples rather than to attract the multitude. If the church is going to make an impact in North America, new strategies are needed to make disciples, deploy them, and send them out as harvest workers. Cell church ministry offers exciting possibilities for those doing ministry in North America.

## Chapter Two

# Obstacles to North American Cell Church

**"I** **'m convinced that cell-based ministry** is the most biblical model," a church leader said to me. "But why is it so hard for the North American church to really grasp it?" I've heard similar comments since coming back from Ecuador. To rephrase this question in a positive light, What's it going to take to see the cell church model come to life in North America? By looking at the following obstacles to cell ministry in North America, my goal is to provide answers and tools for people ministering in North America. Though distinct obstacles do confront those in North American cell ministry, solutions also abound.

## Obstacle #1: Church as a Sunday morning event

As I sat next to Nancy on the plane, she shared with me her testimony. She had received Jesus and begun attending a large evangelical church that faithfully taught God's Word each Sunday. "Over time," she said, "it became painful to smile, walk through the church doors, hear the message, and leave one hour later to resume our family crisis in the car in the church parking lot."

She finally stopped attending the church because she felt like a hypocrite. For Nancy, going to church was hearing the preacher on Sunday. Granted, she could have volunteered for various activities in the church, but she, like so many others, equated "church" with the large group gathering on Sunday morning.

We were hoping that Jim would respond to the challenge of discipleship and join our cell-based church in southern California. He decided to leave, saying, "Joel, once I go to church on Sunday morning, I feel like I'm done with church for the week." He, like so many, wasn't ready for anything beyond Sunday morning.

The North American church is heir of the European immigration that populated this continent. Those who settled this land from Europe brought with them the Reformation view of the church. The definition of the church according to Luther, Calvin, Zwingli, and other reformers (all from Europe) was a *place* where the gospel was rightly preached, the sacraments rightly administered, and church discipline correctly exercised.

Such a definition was light years ahead of the Roman hierarchical view of the church, but it tended to exalt the preacher and convert the rest into hearers.

The church routine we inherited from the Reformers is now well known. Members arrive at church well-dressed (except in California where they might come in short pants!) to hear God's Word. Granted, the Sunday hour includes worship, announcements, offerings, and occasional celebration of the Lord's Supper, but the high note comes when the pastor stands up to preach God's Word from the pulpit. For most North Americans this experience lasts for one and a half hours.

The spectator nature of the church, however, doesn't turn members into ministers or make disciples of the multitudes. It fails to promote the priesthood of all believers, and it overemphasizes the *hearing* of the Word. Though we must rejoice in those who God has called to preach, Scripture tells us that we are all ministers and that God Himself has "made us to be a kingdom and priests to serve his God and Father" (Rev. 1:6).

Most North American seminaries teach potential pastors how to preach, counsel, visit, conduct funerals, weddings, administer the sacraments, and administer the church. Seminary teaching is based on the Reformation view that the church is the place where people gather to hear the preacher.

## The cell church solution

Cell ministry today, therefore, requires a value shift about the very nature of the church. It requires a re-emphasis on the priesthood of all believers ministering to one another through the gifts of the Spirit. Cell-based ministry promotes attendance and ministry in the cell as being equal to the Sunday celebration. Those hearing the Word on Sunday are in life-transforming cell groups during the week that go beyond information to transformation.

The cell-church philosophy, in reality, is a reformation of ecclesiology (the study of the history and theology of the Christian church). Easum reflects on the future church, "The Reformers 'marks of a true church' is out. Church will not be defined as the place where the gospel is rightly preached, the sacraments duly administered, and church discipline exercised. Already, concerns such as house churches, cell groups, warehouse churches, cyber churches . . . are gaining priority."[1]

Preparing the laity to do the ministry is a radical, refreshing change. It rightly emphasizes Paul's direction in Ephesians 4:11–12. Cell groups provide the best atmosphere to prepare and develop laypeople. In this atmosphere laypeople can exercise such skills as listening, caring, speaking, and evangelizing.

---

## Obstacle #2: Church as a building

Church buildings are not inherently bad. The problem arises when the building is equated with the church. When the early church founders spoke of churches, they were referring to gathered communities of believers meeting in the homes of the members. Archeologists find no hint of church buildings before the year AD 150. Yet the church flourished.

The church in China is growing at an unprecedented rate—without a building. Cell churches prioritize the prime real estate of the city—the homes of the people, whose property collectively might be worth millions of dollars.

I believe buildings are neutral entities that can serve the people of God and provide a meeting place to celebrate, receive training, and carry out other activities. Some congregations, however, are bound to their buildings. Slowly, and even imperceptibly, the church becomes equated with the building in which it meets.

After paying large sums of money to erect the building, the church feels obligated to use it continually. When someone talks about cell meetings outside the building, stiff opposition arises. The unspoken feeling is, "We've spent lots of money for this prime piece of real estate and we must use it."

Sometimes churches encourage the cells or small groups to meet in the church building. This is an unfortunate alternative, because cell ministry is designed to penetrate where people, live, work, and breathe. Cell ministry is not a come-and-see strategy but a go-where-people-live strategy. Expecting people to come to the building where the small groups meet defeats a key purpose behind cell ministry—penetrating a lost society for Jesus. One successful cell church pastor said, "The devil wants to trap us within the four walls of the church. Criminals don't care if the policeman is pushing papers—as long as he's not out on the street." [2]

### Financial gridlock

I spoke in a North American church that had great expectations for cell growth. The rallying cry was "One hundred cells by the end of the year," and leaders were pumped up and ready to go.

Then came the building program.

Raising money sapped the strength of the cell ministry because priority was placed on getting people into the Sunday celebration—not the cells—in order to raise money (offerings were taken only in the celebration). After the building was completed, the staff felt drained. When I spoke at the church, they listened politely but truly wondered if they could ever regain the cell momentum, which they had lost during the building program.

The same thing happened in a church where I ministered for many years. The senior leader, knowing that money would be raised through the Sunday worship, paid less attention to cell ministry during the building-construction phase. Through that experience I learned a valuable lesson about taking offerings in the cell groups.

## The cell church solution

I now counsel churches to take offerings in cells as well as in celebration. I've seen too many cell churches de-emphasize cell ministry during times of financial crisis, whether through a building program or economic downturn. The underlying subtle value was, "We must get people to the celebration service so we can raise money."

Let's face it: churches need money to survive, and money furthers kingdom purposes, including the salary of the pastor. If cells are also a source of financial growth, the church will see cell group growth as another source of financial income and have less tendency to ignore cell ministry during a financial crunch.

Another reason to take offerings in the cells is that some people will join a cell group before joining the celebration service. Those not attending the celebration service should be given the opportunity to contribute financially. After all, they're benefiting from the church through the cell group. To those who are not yet ready to attend the celebration service, the cell group is their church.

Buildings won't win the next generation for Jesus. The good news is that cell churches are not limited by buildings. With a true New Testament flavor, they meet from house to house. They fully utilize the collective real estate of houses throughout the city.

## Obstacle #3: Individualism

The cultures in which cell based ministry is exploding are face-to-face, people-oriented cultures that have strong group orientation. Because these majority world cultures think and act as a group, cell ministry seems more comfortable and natural.

North American culture in general focuses on the individual as opposed to the group. Each person is encouraged to think and act individually. There are many positive sides to individualism, including individual dignity, human rights, and personal growth.

The downside of individualism is the tendency toward isolationism and family breakdown. It's estimated that six out of ten children born in the U.S. in the 1990s will live in single-parent households by the time they're eighteen years old.[3] I'm astounded by the number of parents who are even willing to abandon their children in the name of self realization or romantic love (another name for carnal appetites). Some critics, noting the North American propensity toward individualism, have concluded that cell ministry doesn't work in the U.S.

## The cell church solution

Although individualism is a cultural trait and can be a hindrance, cell churches do grow and flourish in North America (see Chapter 5).

Seventy-five million adult Americans, in fact, regularly attend the estimated three million small groups.[4] Church analyst Lyle Schaller, after listing twenty innovations in the modern North American church scene, says that perhaps "the decision by tens of millions of teenagers and adults to place a high personal priority on weekly participation in serious, in-depth, lay-led, and continuing Bible study and prayer groups" is the most important of all.[5]

Individualism, as it relates to small groups in North America, doesn't rule out small-group ministry, but it does give small-group ministry a distinct twist. People who participate in small groups in North America normally don't experience the same "group feeling" as participants in other cultures. But there are also advantages.

First, North Americans are far more willing to share their individual stories and participate deeply in the small group than are people in more group-oriented cultures.

I met with some Chinese cell leaders who complained about the lack of transparency in their groups. "The Chinese culture," they said, "hinders open sharing because it's not culturally appropriate to talk about personal things." Many group-oriented cultures, like the Chinese, struggle with individual sharing and transparency in the cell.

Second, North Americans are increasingly feeling the need for small-group ministry because the isolationism that breeds loneliness has created a new hunger for community in North America. Perhaps the primary drawing card for cell ministry in North America is people's need to belong and relate to others. Unchurched people are increasingly drawn to a cell-based church where intimate relationships are a normal part of church life.

Other individual aspects of small group ministry include the following:

- Each individual is encouraged to apply the Word of God in the group setting.
- Individual cell members are encouraged to help lead the cell. The best cell leaders, in fact, rarely lead the entire cell, allowing volunteers to actively participate.
- Each individual is encouraged to receive discipleship and go through a church-approved training track with the goal of eventually becoming a cell facilitator.

## Obstacle #4: Task orientation

Most cultural studies rank North Americans high on task orientation and low on relationships. Commitment to *getting the job done* is an important part of North American life.

In North America, busyness is a virtue. Idleness is a sin. Lingenfelter and Mayers write, "The social life of task-oriented individuals is often merely an extension of work activity. . . . Task-oriented people consider social activities a drain on their productive time and often prefer the solitude of working alone and uninterrupted. To achieve is more important than to build social relationships, and they are willing to endure social deprivation to reach their goals."[6]

This task orientation is built into the very nature of how North Americans are rewarded. In North America, rewards are granted according to achievement rather than personal relationships. People from group-oriented cultures, on the other hand, achieve success through developing relationships. They find their significance in establishing and maintaining friendships.

### The cell church solution

Many don't realize, however, that cell ministry is also task oriented. While not minimizing the power of small group community and relationship building, it's unwise and even faulty to assume that cell-based ministry is not task oriented.

The fastest-growing worldwide cell churches treat cell ministry in a systematic "task-like" fashion. The cells in these churches are positioned to evangelize, develop leaders, and multiply. Goals are set for cell multiplication. Charts, maps, and financial resources help the cells fulfill their goals and purposes. The cell offices in these growing cell churches reminded me of war-time planning centers rather than cozy fellowship halls. Worldwide cell churches take seriously their work to penetrate the entire city for Jesus Christ. Fellowship happens in the process of fulfilling God's plan.

Cell groups have a clear task to evangelize, develop leaders, and multiply. In my contact with cell churches around the world, I've noticed a constant forward motion. This philosophy allows a church to focus on precise goals and objectives much better than do current church growth strategies.

It's this clarity that makes the cell church strategy doable in any culture, whether in North America or overseas.

Research and experience indicate that fellowship (community) is enhanced when the group is reaching out and winning a lost world for Jesus Christ. Fellowship occurs when members of the group are intimately working together in a loving, small-group atmosphere to reach non-Christians and start new groups.

Small-group ministry is not, as some assume, only for relationally inclined people who are emotionally starved and need a touchy-feely environment. I met with one business person who resisted small-group involvement saying, "I'm just not the touchy-feely type." I responded, "You don't have to be. You'll encourage the group with your own gifts, talents, and personality. When you go through the training track and start facilitating your own cell group, you'll attract people more like yourself."

Granted, cell ministry offers both deep relationships and a clear task of fulfilling the great commission of Jesus Christ. Deep cell community and clear cell goals are not mutually exclusive. They can work in harmony to reach a lost world for Christ.

## Obstacle #5: Busyness

Many people say that cell ministry won't work in North America because of its demands on very busy people. Yes, North Americans are very busy, working eight weeks more per year than the average western European, because working hard is a very important value.[7] Although hard work is, in most cases, a necessity to make a living, we have gone further and have elevated being busy to a virtue, a trait of good character.

Busyness, however, is a relative term and speaks of values more than of a flurry of activity. North Americans are also very busy watching TV because TV watching is an important value. North Americans watch an average of four hours of TV per day. Should we count these hours as *busyness*? Busyness simply means doing things that are considered important. North American busy hours are often directed toward personal priorities.

----

## The cell church solution

A well-developed cell system will give North American church members a reason to dedicate more time and energy and will incite them to a vision beyond themselves—to expect more from God and to attempt greater things for God.

Cell ministry offers an exciting challenge of personal involvement, discipleship, cell leadership, coaching new leaders, and even—for those who want more—someday pastoring a church.

The cell church passion must start in the heart of the lead pastor and key leaders. If the senior minister isn't involved in cell ministry, church members will certainly not give it the time of day. When a pastor gives clear leadership and paints a picture of what God wants, believers will follow as their priorities change and they become willing to fill their hours with different, more enduring busyness.

Some churches try to overcome the busyness barrier by promoting church life as easy and painless. "Come to our church and we won't make you do anything," seems like the promotional edge of some church-growth techniques. Yet having a goal of Sunday attendance, offerings, and occasional involvement in church programs won't win North America for Jesus and will fail to incite church members to go further in their walk with Him.

The busyness barrier can't be overcome by demanding less because this is a compromise to the Christian message. Jesus repeatedly reminded His disciples that following Him would demand everything—not just a few free moments (Luke 14:25–35).

## Obstacle #6: North American culture

One church leader wrote, "I was with a group of pastors the other day. One of the pastors, who is a church planter, said that cell ministry is not working in the American culture and it's been generally set aside here in America. It works in other cultures, just not here." He then asked for my opinion. Many pastors echo this same concern: Cell church might work over there but not here. It's easy to look at the growing cell churches in other cultures and conclude that the primary reason they grow is culturally related.

### The cultures of North America

Culture is defined as the beliefs, customs, practices, and social behavior of a particular nation or people. When talking about a *particular people* we usually think in terms of ethnicity. Yet culture goes beyond ethnicity to include such areas as the cultural differences between the generations.

What works among the baby boomers, for example, probably won't work well among the Generation X crowd. Postmoderns in general are far more open to community and relationships than their predecessors.

The high-tech programs that attracted baby boomers are not as relevant for Generation Next. The emerging church is hungry for Christ-like relationships and reality-based ministry. They want to see Jesus in people before they're ready to "decide" for Jesus.[8]

Generation Next longs for a simpler form of church—one that views ministry in terms of relationally-based New Testament ministry rather than high-tech programs, big-screen TVs, and marketing strategies to grow a church.

North American culture also includes small-town culture, urban culture, and southern culture. Then there's popular culture, corporate/business culture, and church culture.

In addition, North American culture is constantly changing. It's far different now than it was thirty years ago.

---

### A changing North American society[9]

- **Percent of American people raised on small farms:**
  In 1900: 40%    In 1970: 5%

- **Percent of American adults classified as overweight:**
  In 1980: 46%    In 2003: 65%

- **Percent who said it's OK to be overweight:**
  In 1985: 45%    In 2003: 75%

- **Percent of Americans who said they smoke:**
  In 1964: 65%    In 2000: 23%

- **Percent of American children born to unwed mothers:**
  In 1960: 5%    In 2000: 33%

- **Percent of American women with only one child:**
  In 1983: 10%    In 2002: 23%

- **Percent of American women in the job market:**
  In 1973: 51%    In 2000: 71%

- **Percent of college degrees earned by women:**
  In 1960: 34%    In 1997: 56%

---

From the late 1600s until well into the 1900s, the United States and Canada received a flood of immigrants from Europe that laid the foundation for North American ethnic culture. Today, however, a larger and larger proportion of the North American population is coming from Latin America, to the point that in thirty-five years approximately one of every four people in the United States will be of Spanish descent. Due largely to the ethnic influx, the United States is forecast to grow from the current 293 million to 420 million by 2050.[10]

More and more minorities, particularly African Americans and Asians, are entering the ministry. Minority students now make up approximately 25% of the enrollment at seminaries accredited by the Association of Theological Schools, compared with 6% in 1977.[11]

North America must increasingly be seen from the perspective of a great variety of colors and cultural diversity. The white population of California, for example, is now officially a minority race. Los Angeles, like many urban centers, is now brown and black. Even the suburbs have been transformed. Entire suburban neighborhoods are dominated by Vietnamese, Armenians, Chinese, and Koreans. Mayan Indians have recreated urban versions of their villages in the Guatemalan highlands in California.[12]

Beyond ethnicity is the fact that western culture in general, and North America in particular, is increasingly becoming secular. Not only North America but also places like Europe and Australia are now post-Christian or postmodern in their thinking.

In today's secular climate, spiritual revival is lacking in general. I remember one humble pastor standing up at a Christian and Missionary Alliance (CMA) council and saying to his fellow pastors, "Let's just humbly admit that we need help. The church is not growing in North America, and we must simply humble ourselves and cry out to the living God for revival."

The question of North American culture is complex. When people simplistically say, "Cells don't work in North American culture," the question must be asked, What aspect of North American culture is being referred to? It's more accurate to say that cell church doesn't work as well among certain segments of a culture in a particular geographical area.

## The cell church solution

Some people look at the success of Bethany World Prayer Center in Louisiana and say, the cell church at Bethany works because it's located in the south.

The fact is, however, that cell churches are flourishing throughout the United States in such diverse places as California, Washington, Arizona, Texas, Louisiana, Georgia, Pennsylvania, Virginia, and New York (see Chapter 5). Rob Reimer, North American cell church pastor, says "The cell church clearly works in the U.S. I'm in New England, a place steeped in tradition, slow to change, and the second least 'churched' region in the U.S., and we've grown from 0 to 425 in less than seven years (50% of the growth has been conversion growth)."

People have very similar cultural questions about cell ministry throughout the world. Lawrence Khong, senior pastor of the 10 000-member cell church in Singapore, said, "When cell church was introduced from the USA to Singapore, people in Singapore said,

'It won't work here: culturally it's American.' When cell church was introduced from Singapore into Malaysia, people responded, 'It won't work here: culturally it's Singaporean.' And when cell church ideas were taken back from Singapore to the USA, some folk said, 'It won't work here: culturally it's too Singaporean.'"[13]

Cell ministry—with its flexibility and its personal, customized-to-the-community nature— provides the perfect opportunity for small groups to reach out and minister to these diverse people groups.

---

In the midst of major obstacles, opportunities often present themselves. Paul could say to the church in Corinth, "I will stay on at Ephesus until Pentecost, because a great door for effective work has opened to me, and there are many who oppose me" (1 Cor. 16:8–9). Those who opposed Paul didn't hinder him from walking through the open door. Cell ministry in North America has unique challenges. But there are also many open doors to spread the net of community life and relational evangelism in an increasingly impersonal culture.

## Chapter Three

# Growing Healthy Churches

**T**he book *Natural Church Development,* by Christian Schwarz, exploded on the church world in 1996 as the foremost *worldwide* statistical study on why churches grow. For the initial study, Schwarz and fellow researchers at Natural Church Development (NCD) collected 4.2 million pieces of data from churches all over the world to determine the reasons for church growth.[1]

They identified a list of eight quality-related characteristics common in all growing churches and then determined that churches that scored 65 or higher on all eight characteristics were growing both in quality and quantity.[2] These are the eight quality-related characteristics:

- Empowering leadership: leaders of growing churches empower others and emphasize the priesthood of all believers.
- Gift-oriented ministry: growing churches utilize the giftedness of each believer.
- Passionate spirituality: growing churches are passionate about their relationship with Jesus Christ.
- Functional structures: growing churches are not led by traditions of the past. Their leadership structures are adaptable.
- Inspiring worship: growing churches have dynamic worship services.
- Holistic small groups: growing churches prioritize life-giving cells.
- Need-oriented evangelism: growing churches evangelize through meeting needs of others in practical ways.
- Loving Relationships: growing churches establish caring relationships among the members.

I've been amazed at how many North American churches and denominations are using NCD tools and materials to help their congregations grow naturally, both in quality and quantity. *Natural Church Development* has become a powerful force in North American and in Christ's Church worldwide.

## Cell churches and conventional churches

The big question is whether cell churches are healthier churches than non-cell churches. A statistical study made this comparison.

In 2002, six years after the original NCD study, NCD compared cell churches to non-cell churches.[3] NCD used twenty million pieces of data in this comparative study because their data bank had continued growing from the initial 4.2 million pieces of data in 1996. The 2002 comparative study revealed that cell churches not only grew faster but were far healthier—in every area.

For many this is not surprising because cell churches ask all members to exercise their spiritual muscles and get involved in using their gifts. The findings, nevertheless, are quite encouraging to those who are doing cell ministry and even for those considering it. I quote here the summary finding sent directly from the NCD data center, where the study originated:

Comparing the NCD scores of cell churches and non-cell churches showed that cell churches overall scored significantly higher in all areas than non-cell churches. Combined cell church scores averaged 59 while combined non-cell church scores averaged 45. Not surprisingly, Inspiring Worship showed the smallest difference (8 points higher for cell churches) and Holistic Small Groups showed the most difference (25 points higher for cell churches). Significantly, even churches that say they would focus on small groups over large group worship still had better scores for large group worship. This finding indicates that cells don't detract from corporate worship—they add to it. Additionally, the rate of church planting—in spite of the fact that the cell church movement has seemed to focus on getting larger rather than on planting more churches—would seem to indicate that multiplication is in fact in the genetic code. Cell churches averaged 2.5 churches planted compared to 1.9 churches planted for non-cell churches. Finally, the study showed that cell churches demonstrated an average growth rate almost double that of non-cell churches.[4]

Because I wasn't sure how NCD defined a cell church, I communicated directly with Christoph Schalk, the principal researcher behind NCD and this particular study. Schalk told me that their research team classified a cell church as a church with a score of 65 or higher in holistic small groups and with more than 75% of worship attendance in small groups. For the sake of emphasis, let me say this another way: in churches labeled cell churches by this study, more than 75% of those who attended weekend worship also attended holistic small groups during the week, and these churches excelled in holistic small groups by scoring higher than 65 in the NCD testing.[5]

This still doesn't define, however, what a holistic small group is according to NCD. The answer to this question can be found in the book *Natural Church Development*, where the characteristics of a holistic small group include the following:

- Emphasis on the application of biblical truth that leads to transformation. People in these small groups have the liberty to bring up issues that apply to daily life.
- Exercise of spiritual gifts within the small group.
- Priority of small groups as being just as important as the celebration service. The small group, in other words, is not simply a programmatic extension of the celebration service. Schwarz uses the term "mini-church" to describe a holistic small group.
- Multiplication. Multiplication stood out as the key factor in healthy, growing churches. Schwarz says, "If we were to identify any one principle as the most important . . . then without a doubt it would be the multiplication of small groups." Schwarz continues, "Continuous multiplication of small groups is a universal church growth principle."[6]

The NCD definition of a holistic small group is very close to the cell definition given in the introduction of this book. I also like their definition of a cell church and believe it's an excellent starting point. I have appreciated the ministry of NCD, and I'm encouraged to see that their extensive research is confirming that cell church ministry is a healthy strategy for church growth.[7]

This study is exciting because it provides statistical evidence that cell churches—whether in North America, Europe, or Africa—are not only healthier but also are growing faster. This information gives hope to those who have doubted that the cell-church strategy could bring qualitative and quantitative growth to their churches. For those planting a church or whose congregation is in transition from a conventional church to a cell church, this study is a reminder that cell church ministry will actually give a boost to celebration worship, church planting, and overall growth.

Since twenty million pieces of data were used in this comparative study, it certainly should be taken seriously and applied accordingly. Embarking on the cell church journey takes prayer, planning, and persistence. The NCD study should be a huge encouragement—no matter how many obstacles—to press ahead until the breakthrough comes.

## Back to making disciples

I believe God is stirring His church to focus on making disciples who make disciples. He's raising up a church that grows from the inside out—from the core to the crowd.

The beauty of the cell church approach is that it fulfills Christ's great commission to make disciples and allows a pastor to concentrate on building healthy members. When this happens, I've noticed that the celebration service increases—quite naturally.

More and more pastors and churches are focusing on developing holistic small groups that produce disciples through evangelism and multiplication. These same churches are reorganizing the work of pastors and lay leaders from managing church tasks and programs to pastoring networks of small group leaders.

More than a decade ago, Bill Hull wrote a book called *The Disciple Making Pastor*. Hull critiqued America's Sunday attendance strategies as being totally inadequate and emphasized the need to make disciples. I resisted Hull's teaching, thinking he lacked church growth insight. At that time, I primarily judged church growth success by how many were seated in a church in the worship service.

Yet now I applaud the concept of growing a church from the inside out and measuring success by disciples made and sent forth. The only *command*, in fact, of Christ's great commission was to make disciples. The rest of the verbs in Matthew 28:18–20 are not in the command form but in the participle form. Jesus literally said, "having gone, make disciples." (Matt. 28:18).

Concentrating on making disciples through cell church ministry requires a new vision that demands personal involvement. First, the senior pastor must pay the price by modeling small-group ministry to key leaders and church members.

Second, church members must pay the price by actively participating in a cell as part of the normal church commitment. Cell involvement is just as important, if not more so, than celebration attendance.

Taking the time to build a God-honoring church that is making disciples is not easy. But Jesus did tell us to count the cost. The NCD study challenges us to grow a church from the inside out—one that produces lasting, fruitful growth.[8] Growing healthy churches through the cell church strategy is vital to get the North American church back on track. Thankfully, many churches in North America are already successfully implementing the cell church strategy. They can inspire and give insight to those who want to follow in their steps.

## Chapter Four

# Cell Church Models

**A**s I've seen what churches in North America are doing to develop strong cell groups, I have found that they all embrace common cell principles. Yet very few of them follow a specific model or pattern. They do things in distinctive, culturally relevant ways. They discover what works in their own settings and then apply the principles to fit the context. Some have erroneously thought they must follow a model developed by David Cho, Carl George, Ralph Neighbour, or others to develop cells well. But the evidence does not support this.

Instead of following one model, I encourage churches to embrace the Radical Middle. Before I explain what I mean by the Radical Middle, allow me to give a brief history of the small-group strategies current on the North American scene.[1]

## The Korean cell church movement

When I first heard David Cho speak on the wonders of cell church ministry in 1984, my life was transformed. At that time, Cho had 500 000 members in Yoido Full Gospel Church, and he gave testimony after testimony about how he was able to effectively pastor each member of his church through the cell system.

I listened to Cho's tapes over and over and even taught my congregation according to Cho's model. On numerous occasions, Cho and his cell ministry inspired me to think outside the box.

Cho's model paved the way for the cell–celebration philosophy to take root in North America. Many pastors made a pilgrimage to Seoul, South Korea to visit Cho's church and bring back the exciting developments they witnessed.

Cho's model, however, failed to fully transfer to the North American context. The Korean culture is so different that the majority who tried to repeat Cho's small-group system failed.

Although Cho inspired pastors in North America, he didn't give them the nuts and bolts to actually make it work. I speak from personal experience. Although I was greatly encouraged by Cho's book *Successful Home Cell Groups*, the book didn't give me enough information to grow a cell system. Although Cho continued to write extensively, he didn't write another book about the practical details of the cell model.[2]

## The Meta Model

Carl George, author and expert in church growth, adapted Cho's model and made it more relevant to North America. George's book *Prepare Your Church for the Future* demonstrated that the church of the future would be a collection of small groups. He called his new approach the Meta Model. This book had a powerful impact on the North American church scene because George gave fresh, North American terminology to the cell-based concepts that have worked so well overseas.

---

*...the cell church in North America has now gone far beyond those pioneer days. Now there are cell churches that are practically leading the way in how to grow healthy, multiplying churches.*

---

In his second book about the Meta Model, *The Coming Church Revolution*, George showed how far he was ready to adapt cell ministry to North America by saying that small groups included, "Sunday-school classes, ministry teams, outreach teams, worship-production teams, sports teams, recovery groups, and more. . . . Any time sixteen or fewer people meet together, you have a small-group meeting."[3]

Commenting on the Meta Model, David Limiero writes, "The key to understanding George's model is recognizing that your church *already* has existing small groups. These groups might be Sunday school classes, the choir, elders, committees, women's circles, etc."[4]

The weakness, in my opinion, of George's model was defining the cell so loosely that it lost much of its quality. While I commend George's cultural sensitivity to small groups, I believe the quality control of the cell itself suffered under the Meta Model.[5]

Many churches use George's Meta Model because it's a way to quickly adapt a church to small-group ministry, since everything is called a "small group" or "cell." Training and coaching, however, are hard to maintain because the needs of a monthly sports leader, for example, are vastly different from the needs of a weekly multiplying cell group leader.

I've also noticed an adverse effect in churches when all small groups are embraced in the cell system and given equal priority. A cell group, unlike many small groups, includes evangelism, leadership development, and multiplication.

I'm grateful for the Meta Model's cultural sensitivity, though I'm concerned that key cell components were lost.

## The pure, pure, cell church

When Ralph Neighbour's book *Where Do We Go From Here?* appeared in 1990, it forged a powerful cell movement. God used the book in a wonderful way to awaken people to the growth of the worldwide cell church and a cell movement was started.

The cell church owes a lot to Ralph Neighbour for his passion for cell-based evangelism, his emphasis on equipping every cell member, and his ability to fill in a lot of the details that pastors previously didn't understand.

The negative tone of the book, however, pitted cell churches against the church at large. The preface to the 2001 edition of the book admits this and Neighbour even apologizes for his tone.

The faithful in the cell church movement of the early '90s often lacked sensitivity to the rest of Christ's church. One pastor, echoing the sentiment of others said, "I didn't even try to transition my church after reading *Where Do We Go From Here?* because Neighbour said in the book that the North American program-based church was hopeless and couldn't be transitioned."

Though a movement was created, the cell church in North America has now gone far beyond those pioneer days. Now there are cell churches that are practically leading the way in how to grow healthy, multiplying churches.

The image that the cell church is against the conventional church still persists and causes resistance among many when it comes to implementing cell church ministry. Many leaders want the benefits of following cell church principles, but they don't want the label and image of being a "cell church." Often the reason for this resistance is a negative feeling or connotation that the cell church is against all other expressions of Christ's church.

God is raising up a new generation of leaders who are seeking practical solutions for superficiality in the church, acute isolationism among members, and a general lack of growth. These pastors are looking to cell church ministry to grow healthy small groups that emphasize evangelism, community, and leadership development.

## The G12 phenomenon

The International Charismatic Mission (ICM) in Bogota, Colombia, gave a breath of fresh air to the cell church movement in the early '90s when it initiated Groups of Twelve (G12), a new way to multiply cells and care for cell leaders. The G12 vision has now spread to many North American Churches. Some of the most prominent cell churches in the U.S., such as Bethany World Prayer Center, have fully adopted the G12 model.[6]

ICM started in 1986 by following Cho's model one hundred percent. It then tweaked Cho's model to fit its own cultural context to make cell church work better there. Some of the excellent adjustments were
- viewing everyone as a potential cell leader
- asking the leader of the mother cell to care for/coach the leader of the daughter cell
- developing a clear, dynamic equipping training track that prepared everyone for ministry
- emphasizing encounter-with-God retreats to ensure freedom from sinful strongholds, believing that holiness brings fruit
- prioritizing prayer and spirituality as keys to future growth

ICM, however, began to promote the G12 model as the new revelation of God, asking people to follow it precisely—to adopt it and not adapt it. The G12 became imbalanced, in my opinion, by asking people to
- commit to following the G12 model exactly[7]
- believe that the number twelve has special significance and even an anointing attached to it

- commit one hundred percent to use only ICM materials[8]
- develop strict homogeneity in cell networks[9]
- have zeal for only one cell model, rather than seeing themselves as part of a wider cell church family

God has wonderfully used the G12 cell church movement to fine-tune the worldwide cell church. The cell church movement welcomes the principles—but resists the mentality that says, "This model is the new revelation from God and must be followed precisely."

I've noticed that G12ers often use the incredible growth of ICM as proof of God's blessing. Yet the Elim cell church in El Salvador is probably larger than ICM and growing just as fast. Elim, however, uses a geographical 5x5 model that is totally different from the G12 model.

The point is that principles, rather than models, help cell churches grow. Principles apply across a wide variety of cultures and churches. Models are harder to implement and far more restrictive.[*]

---

*The word radical means that cell ministry will often go against the grain of conventional thinking that says Sunday morning is church.*

---

## The Radical Middle and Cell Church Solutions

Many North American leaders today find themselves in a place that I'm labeling the Radical Middle. They are trying to find a balance between cell quality and cultural relevance. These leaders greatly desire to maintain the key components of cell ministry, but they're just as passionate to make sure it actually works in North America (not just ideally or theoretically working).

The term Radical Middle highlights the radical nature of cell ministry yet also proclaims the need for practicality—it must work. The word *radical* means that cell ministry will often go against the grain of conventional thinking that says Sunday morning *is* church.

---

[*] For more on the Elim Church see my 2004 book *Passion and Persistence* at **www.cellchurchsolutions.com.**

The *middle* is important because the sensitive cell church leader must make sure that the congregation is following and not left behind in a trail of idealism. Some pastors are very radical about cell ministry but just can't seem to lead their congregations to follow along. The Radical Middle declares that great cell ministry will eventually work to make disciples, grow congregations, and plant new churches. Solutions, rather than idealism, will ultimately win the day.

I didn't invent the Radical Middle,[10] nor am I the only one promoting it. I see the Radical Middle as a place on the small-group continuum where many leaders find themselves. More and more leaders want to concentrate on making disciples who make disciples. Their passion is to make cell church work in their own context.

Leaders in the Radical Middle resist the tendency to water down the definition of a true cell, fiercely desiring to maintain the quality control. Yet, these same leaders don't want all the baggage associated with the "pure, pure" cell church.

They simply want to know how to make disciples, develop leaders, evangelize more effectively, and eventually plant new cell churches. They want purity and practicality. This is the same thing Cell Church Solutions promotes—purity and practicality.

Three concepts define the heart of the Radical Middle. Beyond these three, flexibility reigns.

## 1. Guidance by the senior leader

The senior pastor, or senior leader, must guide the cell-group vision. Other leaders can help a lot, and various cell champions are mentioned in the pages of this book.[11] Yet the vision and overall leadership belong to the lead pastor.[12] Dale Galloway, one of the pioneer cell church pastors in North America and author of many cell books, writes, "No matter who introduces small-group ministry into a church, that ministry will only go as far as the Senior Pastor's vision for it. The people will watch the Senior Pastor to see if small-group ministry is important."[13]

Key members can influence the senior pastor to catch the vision, yet ultimately cell church ministry succeeds or fails by whether senior leadership is promoting and living it. The bottom line is that sheep follow the shepherd.

Actions speak much louder than words, and this is especially true in cell-based ministry.

I encourage senior leaders to grow in their knowledge of cell-based ministry by reading the literature, visiting cell churches, and being involved in the battle. I'm always impressed when a senior pastor actually leads a cell group, or at least has recently led a cell group. This shouts to those around him that the senior pastor is wrestling with the same issues. He is learning and growing in cell ministry.[†]

## 2. Clear definition of a cell

The strength of the cell church resides in the quality of the cell. Since the cell is the crown jewel of the cell church, watering down the cell to the lowest denominator must be avoided at all costs. Though there is a great flexibility with regard to homogeneity, lesson material, order of a cell meeting, location of the meeting, and degree of participation, it's exceedingly important to maintain quality control of the following aspects:

- regularity (weekly cell meetings are the norm in all the worldwide cell churches and this should be maintained)
- penetration (cells meet outside the church building to penetrate the world where people live, move, and breathe)
- evangelism (evangelism should be prioritized)
- community (people are dying for relationships and cell groups offer close community)
- discipleship/spiritual growth (cell groups offer pastoral care and spiritual growth for those attending)
- multiplication (the goal of the cell should be to develop the next leader to continue the process through multiplication)

Labeling cell groups as everything that is small and a group lowers the quality of the cell and ultimately the quality of the entire cell church.

---

† **www.cellchurchsolutions.com/articles/churchLeaders/seniorPastorsRole.htm** talks about the senior pastor's role in the cell church.

Defining a cell group according to quality components has nothing to do with legalism but everything to do with desiring that those in the cell have a qualitative experience. To call everything a cell in the name of *creativity* is like a pastor encouraging members to do whatever and go wherever they want for Sunday celebration, rather than come to the weekly celebration church service.[14]‡

## 3. Cells as the base of the church

Making cells the base of the church means not allowing other programs to dominate the church schedule. Although many cell churches have other ministries, they do ask the people involved in those additional ministries to actively participate in the cells. In this way, cells remain the base of the church.

Growing the cell infrastructure is the number one priority in the cell church. Sunday attendance growth comes as the result of growing the cell infrastructure—making disciples who make disciples.‡‡

## Flexibility

Apart from these three key components, flexibility reigns in the Radical Middle. There's liberty to experiment, create, and adapt cell church principles to the church's context, people, and reality.

The Radical Middle sees the cell as the crown jewel and tries to base church life around it. The only way to make cells central is through promotion of it by the senior pastor. Yet, every church will have a different way of doing it. I love to visit cell churches that demonstrate creativity. It shows me that the senior pastor and ministry team have done their homework to discern what works for them.

John Wesley is a great example of adapting small-group concepts to establish his own cell church system (the method of the Methodists) more than 250 years ago. Wesley had an "an unusual capacity to accept suggestions and

---

‡ www.cellchurchsolutions.com/articles/basics/whatIsACell.htm talks about the definition of a cell.

‡‡ www.cellchurchsolutions.com/articles/churchLeaders/integratingMinistries.htm talks about what it actually means to make cells the base of the church. See also www.cellchurchsolutions.com/articles/churchLeaders/integration.htm for more on this topic.

to adopt and adapt methods from various quarters."[15] George Hunter says, "He learned from exposure to the home groups that the Lutheran Pietist leader Philip Jacob Spener developed to fuel renewal and outreach, and Wesley learned particularly from the Moravians. Wesley also learned from Anabaptist groups and from the occasional 'societies' within the church of England, so his group movement was eclectic Protestant."[16]

In the Radical Middle, no one model is forced on all cell churches. No one training track is touted as the only way to train leaders. No one coaching structure is promoted to the exclusion of all others. If it works, use it. If it doesn't work, don't. In the Radical Middle, homogeneous and heterogeneous cells both work great, and one type is not promoted to the absolute exclusion of the other. No one cell meeting order or lesson plan is made to seem like the only one. Many suggestions are made, but they don't make up the core identity of cell ministry—what is and what isn't a cell church.

The movement of the Radical Middle seeks to discover how cell ministry *actually* works, rather than how it *should* work. A key priority is to discover principles from churches that are making it happen.

The Radical Middle sees the need for North American cell-based ministry to team up with churches around the world to promote a core-to-crowd strategy and to support the churches that are doing so. The ministry of Cell Church Solutions promotes the Radical Middle through resources, coaching, and teaching.

## Chapter Five

# Evidence You Can't Deny

**stayed away from cell church circles until 1996.** I wasn't
impressed with cell church rhetoric; I even resisted it. Something changed
radically in 1996 that made me a cell church enthusiast. The difference? I visited
cell churches. I saw the power of cell evangelism and multiplication. I witnessed
the intimate pastoral care provided by the cell leaders. I realized that this was
what I was looking for in church life and ministry.

I hear a similar yearning in pastors today. They don't want the rhetoric, but
they do want to see reality. I hear them say continually, "Where are the healthy
cell churches in North America?"

North Americans are pragmatic. It's part of their cultural heritage. They want
to see, experience, and analyze healthy cell churches before they're willing to
make the leap. In this chapter we look at these cell churches, what they're doing,
and what we can learn from them.

Admittedly, the churches chosen in this chapter reflect my bias. I've picked
them because I'm personally familiar with them, having ministered in them or
known the senior pastor, or can verify the results. I've held seminars, in fact,
in seventeen of the forty-four churches listed here. I'm sure I've missed many
great cell churches. Touch Outreach has listed close to 300 North American cell
churches at www.touchusa.org for those looking for more information.[1]

The churches in this chapter represent various denominations and networks:
Assemblies of God, American Baptist, Calvary Chapel, Church of Christ, Church
of God, Christian and Missionary Alliance, Covenant, Dove Christian Fellowship,
Free Methodist, Lutheran, Nazarene, Southern Baptist, Pentecostal, Pentecostal
Free Will Baptist, United Methodist, Vineyard, and Wesleyan.

Nineteen of the churches are non-denominational. Some of the churches
would be considered charismatic while others would not use that label.

The thirty-nine U.S. churches are found in eighteen states. That they are dispersed throughout the U.S. strongly suggests that the cell church can work anywhere in the U.S.

Three of the five Canadian churches are located in the province of Ontario; the other two are 2000 miles to the west in the province of British Columbia. For further treatment of the cell movement in Canada, I recommend the book *Church without Walls*, edited by Michael Green, specifically the first chapter, titled "Cell Church in Canada."[2]

I didn't pick these churches based on their Natural Church Development scores because I didn't want to exclude churches that had not submitted to NCD testing.[3] I strongly suspect, however, that their scores would be well over 65% in holistic small groups and that more than 75% of the worshippers would be in small groups during the week. Some of them, in fact, have more people in cells than in celebration.

None of these churches is perfect. The perfect cell church doesn't exist. On a scale of one to ten, I would place most of them at eight or nine. All of them are in transition and would tell you that they haven't arrived.

Another limitation is that the scope of this book doesn't allow me to include cell churches in other western contexts, such as Europe or Australia. One of my favorite cell churches is in Zurich, Switzerland, pastored by my good friend Werner Kniessel.

The churches listed here exemplify church health, not necessarily the largest Sunday celebration attendance in North America. I have purposely avoided arranging them according to size to avoid "number" comparisons.

Some of the churches on this list have chosen to emphasize cell church planting rather than grow into one huge cell church. I personally think this is the best option.[4]

When describing certain churches, I use the term G12 to show how the church cares for cell leaders. G12 simply means Groups of Twelve and is a way to coach cell leaders that César Castellanos developed in 1990. G12 patterns itself after how Jesus cared for his twelve disciples.*

---

* www.cellchurchsolutions.com/articles/coaching/understandingG12.htm talks about the G12 movement. I've written two books on this topic that can be purchased at www.cellchurchsolutions.com or by calling **1-888-344-CELL**.

## Antioch Community Church

Antioch, TX

Pastor Jimmy Seibert, non-denominational

**Facts:** 135 cells; 2000 worship attendance, 30+ church planting teams

www.antiochcc.net

Pastor Jimmy Seibert, while college pastor at Highland Baptist Church, pioneered student-led cell ministry on the Baylor University Campus in Waco, Texas. It grew to some 600 students on four campuses.[5] In 1999 Antioch Community Church was sent out from Highland Baptist Church as a cell church under the leadership of Seibert.

Wherever I go in North America, I keep hearing about the effectiveness of cell ministry at Antioch Community Church. As I've considered the key strength of this church, I've noticed a primary principle: multiplication. This church teaches and practices the multiplication of groups, leaders, churches, and missionaries. With the multiplication of disciples as the core principle, Antioch Community Church is an exciting blend of cell growth, church planting, and missions. This church is exemplifying the power of cell-based ministry in a North American context.

---

## Bethany World Prayer Center

Baker, LA

Pastor Larry Stockstill, non-denominational

**Facts:** 1350 cells, 8000 worship attendance, 1000+ church plants worldwide[6]

www.bethany.com

Bethany World Prayer center is the most fully formed cell church in North America, in my opinion. Bethany's pastors have researched cell church worldwide and since 1996 have hosted yearly cell church conferences. Stockstill's book *The Cell Church* stimulates faith and vision to make cell church a reality in North America.[7] I constantly recommend it to inspire churches to press on in the cell strategy.

Bethany attracts thousands of pastors to its yearly cell conferences and more recently has adopted the G12 model of cell church ministry, following the pattern of the International Charismatic Mission, a cell church in Bogota, Colombia. Bethany continues to plant cell churches worldwide.

---

## Big Bear Christian Center

Big Bear City, CA
Pastor Jeff Tunnell, non-denominational
**Facts:** 20 cells, 200 worship attendance, 1 church plant
www.bigbearchristiancenter.com

This growing cell church is located in a mountain community of 5700 (24 000 in the surrounding area). I've heard people say that cell ministry works only in bustling urban environments. Big Bear Christian Center (BBCC) finds itself in just the opposite environment, yet God is doing great things through the cell ministry.

Since 2000 Tunnell has patiently steered the church through transition to the cell-driven strategy, adapting cell principles to fit the context of Big Bear City. BBCC highlights prayer as the guiding star, emphasizes a rotating preaching team, and has a growing vision to make a world impact through cell ministry.

---

## Camino Real Christian Fellowship

San Antonio, TX
Pastor Ernie Hinojosa, Lutheran (ELCA)
**Facts:** 20 cells, 125 worship attendance, 2 satellite centers
www.mycaminoreal.com

Pastor Ernie Hinojosa planted an innovative Lutheran cell church in San Antonio, Texas, in 2001. The church's special calling is to minister to the needs of San Antonio's inner city community. The church emphasizes the power of prayer and intercession as the key focal points for church growth. The goal is to start at least one cell in each zip code of San Antonio.

This will be accomplished by multiplying cell groups that are part of Camino Real but also by multiplying cell-based satellite ministries in San Antonio. To date, Camino Real has planted a satellite ministry targeting postmodern young adults near the city's downtown art district. This satellite, started as a single cell group of Camino Real, has grown into a full-fledged satellite ministry with five cells.

Camino Real also has recently begun developing a Spanish–English bilingual outreach ministry, started from three Camino Real cell groups. Camino Real believes that, as it multiplies cells of its own and plants other cell-based ministries in the city, it will eventually reach an entire city for Christ.

---

## Celebration Church

New Orleans, LA
Pastor Dennis Watson, Southern Baptist
**Facts:** 120 cells, 1650 worship attendance, 37 church plants
(12 in U.S. and 25 worldwide)
www.celebrationchurch.org

Pastor Dennis Watson led his church's transition to cell-based ministry in 1995 by personally leading the first pilot cell group. God has now granted them more than 100 cells, and the church is at the forefront of the cell movement, even hosting an annual cell church conference.

Celebration Church sees itself as a missionary church, possessing a vision of starting cell-based churches in Louisiana and around the world. They value cell-based ministry as the best way to develop leaders who will penetrate the diverse cultures of New Orleans. The church is also preparing leaders from Africa, Latin America, and Asia to take the gospel back to their home countries.

## Celebration Church, City of Champions

Columbia, MD

Bishop Bob Davis, Church of God (Formerly Long Reach Church of God)

**Facts:** 100 cells, 1800 worship attendance, 7 church plants

www.longreachchurchofgod.org

Bob Davis, a founding member of this church who became pastor a year later, has been at the forefront of the cell church movement since moving this congregation through the transition to a cell church approach fifteen years ago. Davis has coached many pastors in cell church ministry, sharing the insights he's learned in his own church.

High on the priority list in this church is the training track. The church has walked many believers from conversion to maturity through it. Davis writes about the training track: "We have seen God deliver His people from all kinds of life-dominating sins (drugs, spousal and child abuse, homosexuality, marital problems, financial problems, and more) without specific counseling for their particular problem."

This church has effectively reached the Baltimore and Columbia, Maryland, and Washington, DC region for the past thirty-one years.

## Central Christian Assembly

Baltimore, MD

Pastor Terry Kirk, Assemblies of God

**Facts:** 50 cells, 700 worship attendance, 1 church plant

www.Central-Christian.net

Pastor Terry Kirk surrendered his life to Jesus in 1972 after facing hardship growing up in the hills of West Virginia and having experienced several tragic family events. A few months later he was baptized in the Holy Spirit.

God called him into the ministry, and one of the key influences in his life was David Cho (at that time he was Yonggi Cho). During a church growth conference in Atlanta, Georgia, in 1978, God used Cho to ignite a passion in Kirk's heart for cell ministry. In 1983, when Kirk started Central Christian in Baltimore, he finally had the chance to practice the cell vision God had given him five years earlier.

The church has adjusted and adapted cell principles to their own culture and context. They would love to say that their cells were exploding, but they have seriously taken the advice of Karen Hurston, who said, "Just keep plodding, the breakthrough will come." I was impressed with this church's desire to press ahead with the vision that God has given them to reach Baltimore through cell-based ministry.

---

## Champaign Vineyard

Champaign, IL
Pastor Happy Layman, Vineyard
**Facts:** 100 cells, 1500, 4 church plants
www.vineyardchampaign.org

Senior pastor Happy Layman was one of the early cell church pioneers. He, along with Jim Egli, provided training and materials for cell-based ministry in the '90s. Egli, cell church author, earned his PhD studying cell churches around the world and then returned to Champaign Vineyard in 2001 to spearhead the cell ministry there.

The church has grown from 25 cells to 100 (in addition to 25 youth small groups). They are using the Alpha course alongside cell ministry to effectively reach out. The church has increasingly become cell driven as Layman recently made the decision to train all of the staff to coach cell groups. Most of the staff were already leading cells, but their new assignment allows them to pastor the entire church through the cell structure. Egli continues to be the cell champion, under Layman. Champaign Vineyard is fast becoming a shining model of cell-based ministry in North America.

## Christ Fellowship

Fort Worth, TX

Jamey Miller, non-denominational

**Facts:** 25 cells, 300 worship attendance, 9 church plants

www.christfellowship.org

Christ Fellowship, founded in 1993, was not content with simply multiplying cell groups. The church also felt called to plant churches in North America and beyond. Pastor Jamey Miller writes, "We believe that our call to cultivate life-giving cell groups and church plants is rooted in God's plan for His glory on the earth."

The cell-church-planting emphasis flows from the belief that living things multiply. Cell groups multiply through Christ's living presence, and then Christ continues to reach out through church planting. Miller writes, "There's nothing like cell life to bring people into ministry opportunities that cultivate readiness for church planting in another context."

When I met Miller, I was thrilled to hear about his worldwide cell-church-planting vision.

## Church Without Walls

Gastonia, NC

Pastor Steve McCranie, non-denominational

**Facts:** 6 cells, 95 worship attendance

www.thechurchwithoutwalls.org

Pastor Steve McCranie ministered in a traditional Baptist Church for 20 years before starting the Church Without Walls. He now realizes how much easier it is to plant a cell church than try to move an aging one through the transition to cell church. McCranie launched into cell-based ministry in 2000.

The excitement about this church can be seen in its web site— one of the best cell church web sites I've ever seen. The church is not large but it's healthy. Those in the celebration are also in a cell and vice-versa. It's truly a church without walls.

---

## Clearpoint

Houston, TX
Pastor Jay Firebaugh, Southern Baptist
**Facts:** 50 cells, 800 worship attendance
www.ghg.net/clearpoint

Pastor Jay Firebaugh is a leading voice in the cell church world, having specialized in cell leader coaching for many years.[8]

Firebaugh also understands that relationships are the key to making cell ministry work. Clearpoint exemplifies relational evangelism through small-group ministry. Many of Clearpoint's cells have penetrated the unsaved community.

The church continues to influence pastors and churches doing cell ministry across North America. It has supported several churches that were planted in other parts of the world.

---

## Coastal Church

Vancouver, BC, Canada
Pastors David and Cheryl Koop, non-denominational
**Facts:** 35 cells, 700 worshippers
www.coastalchurch.org

In October 1993, a group of Bible school students began witnessing and preaching Jesus on the streets of Vancouver. Pastors Dave and Cheryl Koop, leaders of this student group, eventually planted a church in 1994 called Coastal Church. The church is located in one of the most densely populated and unchurched areas of Canada—only 2% of the population attend church.

The church tried various approaches to reach the community but found that only the cell church model would reach and hold the harvest in this high-rise community. In 2003, for example, the church baptized ninety-one people in nearby English Bay (located in the Pacific Ocean a few blocks away) and then discipled them through the cell system. Heavily influenced by Ralph Neighbour and David Cho, Coastal Church has built and adapted its cell structure over the years.

More than thirty-five nations are represented in this congregation. Some of the cells, in fact, are led in the mother languages of those represented in the congregation. A key value at Coastal Church is missions. One way they engage in missions is to prepare, train, and send harvest workers back to the countries they came from (a large percentage of the congregation is first-generation Christian). I was thrilled to hear that Dave still leads a cell—one of the marketplace cells that meet at lunch time. The church was not only born in a cell in 1994, but the senior pastor still leads one. Koop is doing what Paul said to the Corinthians, "Follow my example, as I follow the example of Christ" (1 Cor. 11:1).

---

## Community Covenant Church

Santa Barbara, CA
Pastor Doug Grimes, Covenant
**Facts:** 30 cells, 500 worshippers
www.community-covenant.org

In 1992 Pastors Dennis Wadley and Jeff Shaffer began moving a dying seventy-member church through the transition to cell-based ministry. Promoting principles over models, the church has steadily grown. The church's vision is clearly stated on its web site: "Like the human body, which is made up of billions of cells (the basic unit of life), the life of Community Covenant is found in its cell groups (small groups of people living out community)."

Community Covenant Church exists in a college community and is seeking to use the cell model to equip people for a lifetime of ministry. Using the cell model of equipping ministers, the church seeks to be a mission outpost that will send people throughout the world connected to God, one another, and to those who are on their journey to Christ. A part of their future vision is to build a school of equipping that will develop ministers in the community who will influence the world for Jesus Christ.

In 2003, Dennis and Susan Wadley, exemplifying what they wanted others to follow, moved to South Africa to serve as missionaries to those who are suffering as a result of the AIDS pandemic. They work with Bridges of Hope, an organization they founded (www.bridges-of-hope.org).

---

## Cornerstone Church & Ministries

Harrisonburg, VA
Senior Pastor Gerald Martin, non-denominational
**Facts:** 125 cells, 1125 worship attendance in 8 network churches and church plants, 1350 total membership[9]
www.cornerstonenet.org

Cornerstone Church & Ministries International (CCMI) is an apostolic network of cell churches and ministries committed to church growth, church planting, and cross-cultural missions.

The church's goal is multiplication at every level: believers multiplying believers, cell groups multiplying cell groups, churches multiplying churches, and networks multiplying networks.

Martin, now operating in the apostolic role, is one of the stalwarts of North American cell-based ministry, having worked closely with Ralph Neighbour for many years. I've been impressed with how Cornerstone has remained on the cutting edge of cell church ministry over the long haul. Their training track is one of the best available today.

Cornerstone has not adopted the G12 care structure in its entirety. Rather they've adapted and fine-tuned it to fit their own culture and context.

## CrossBridge Community Church

San Antonio, TX

Pastor Kirk Freeman

**Facts:** 23 cells, 400 worship attendance

www.crossbridgecommunitychurch.com

In April 2003, Kirk Freeman started this contemporary church. The core value of CrossBridge Community Church (CBCC) is to build community through multiplying life groups.

The church is located in a growing part of north San Antonio. The CBCC celebration attracts many unconnected, unchurched people. Freeman envisions the day when the life groups do most of the connecting and outreach in the community.

The life groups, organized geographically, are designed to reach out to neighbors and friends who live in the same community. Freeman leads his own cell group and highlights the advantages of geographically designed cells: "People in my life group also are in my subdivision. We already shared common schools, shopping patterns, income levels, plus we saw each other regularly through the week." The life group uses the Sunday message as the lesson, trying to integrate as much as possible.

## CrossPoint Community Church

Tucson, AZ

Pastor Jim Corley, CMA

**Facts:** 15 cells, 145 worship attendance, 2 church plants

www.CrossPointer.com

Cell-based ministry flows in the veins of Jim Corley, founding pastor of CrossPoint. Corley spearheaded small groups in a large church in Dayton, Ohio, before planting CrossPoint.

Corley's vision goes beyond his own church. The church's mission statement is to plant twenty-one congregations of five small groups or more by December 2012. They are now preparing to plant their third congregation.

I've been impressed with Corley's capacity to develop leaders who develop leaders. He also has an uncanny ability to pay for building space through daycare facilities. His strategy is to meet a community need (daycare), pay for the building, and develop relationships with non-Christian daycare families through cell-based ministry.

## Crossroads UMC Church

Pittsburgh, PA
Pastor Dr. Steve Cordle, United Methodist
**Facts:** 60 cells, 1000 worship attendance
www.crossroadsumc.org

Crossroad UMC exemplifies to North America that cell church ministry is a viable option and works here just like it does overseas.

Dr. Steve Cordle wrote his dissertation on small-group ministry and understands the concepts very well. In 1994, he planted Crossroads from scratch, and the church has now grown to more than 1000 in Sunday attendance. Cordle has increasingly focused his church along the cell church path, birthing sixty cell groups in the process. Cordle understands the need to produce disciples who are producing disciples.

Cordle recently wrote a book called *The Church in Many Houses: Reaching Your Community through Cell-based Ministry* (Abingdon, 2005), and I highly recommend it. Cordle is one of the partners at Cell Church Solutions and is available for coaching pastors: www. CellChurchSolutions.com.

## Cypress Creek Church

Wimberley, TX
Pastor Rob Campbell, non-denominational
**Facts:** 104 cells, 1100 worship attendance, 42 church plants and partner churches
www.cypresscreekchurch.com

I've taken two groups of pastors to Cypress Creek Church (CCC) since 2002 to give them an introduction and initiation to the North American cell church.

Pastor Rob Campbell started CCC in 1993, recruiting a prayer pastor as the first staff person. Not only has CCC seen incredible local church growth through cell ministry, but this church is committed to planting cell churches worldwide. CCC also has the best youth and college-and-career cells that I've seen in the U.S. (all meeting weekly outside the church).

Campbell's church has adapted the G12 model to fit the North American context. Campbell's exciting book, *Dance with me, Daddy* tells the story of CCC as well as his own story. Campbell is one of the partners connected at Cell Church Solutions and is available for coaching pastors: www.CellChurchSolutions.com.

## Door of Hope Church

Fairbanks, AK
Pastor Dr. Al Woods, non-denominational
**Facts:** 70 cells, 1000 worship attendance
www.doorofhopechurch.org

As a long-time cell seminar teacher, Dr. Al Woods believes and preaches that principles precede structure and practices respond to culture.

Armed with principles, Woods has skillfully guided Door of Hope to be a leading cell church in North America. The web site states, "Door of Hope Church is a cell-based church, which means our relationships with one another in small groups form our church structure. Cells and clusters of cells are our framework for leadership, resourcing missions and ministries, communication, and opportunity. Most importantly, cells have proven to be the place where new members and ministers are birthed and developed."

Door of Hope fundamentally affirms the cell church paradigm while uniquely adapting it to one of America's most isolated, transient, diverse, and youthful communities. The church devotes its resources to help all members discover, activate, develop, and release their Romans 11:29 spiritual gifts and callings.

---

## DOVE Christian Fellowship

Started in Pennsylvania
Founder Larry Kreider, non-denominational
**Facts:** 100+ cell churches
www.dcfi.org

Larry Kreider, founder and international director of the DOVE movement, never intended to start a church. He tried as long as possible to integrate the vanloads of young people whom he and a group of youth had won to Christ into the existing church structures.

Yet, the new wine of God's Spirit burst the old, existing wineskins. Finally, Kreider yielded to God's call on his life and in 1980 started DOVE Christian Fellowship. DOVE is an acronym for "Declaring Our Victory Emmanuel."

This church is perhaps the leading cell church in North America because God has birthed a worldwide cell church planting movement, seminar ministry, and publishing arm through DOVE.

DOVE has planted more than 100 cell churches on five continents. Kreider has based his movement on biblical and cell church principles rather than following one model structure. DOVE cell churches are located in eighteen U.S. states and dispel the myth that cell church doesn't work in North America.

---

## East Hills Alliance Church

Kelso, WA
Pastor Steve Fowler, CMA
**Facts:** 15 cells, 250 worship attendance
www.easthillsalliance.org

Steve Fowler took over this church in 1996, when the church had 70 people. He prayed, studied, and planned for more than four years before making the transition to cell ministry in 2001. He and the elders chose the cell church option because they felt it was the most biblically based strategy.

He changed the church's motto to "Making it hard for the people of Kelso to go to hell." He positioned his small groups to evangelize. From one prototype life group, the life groups multiplied to fifteen, and the church has tripled in both cell and celebration attendance. Fowler and family felt called to become missionaries to China in 2004, but the church continues to grow in cell-based ministry.

---

## Encounter

Memphis, TN
Pastor John Pitman, Church of Christ
**Facts:** 4 cells, 50 worshippers
www.encounterchrist.net

John Pitman, one of the ministers in a Disciples of Christ church, received a mandate from the elders in 2002 to launch a "seeker-friendly" assembly to try to connect with "unchurched" people. Pitman had no desire for such an enterprise but did sense an immense need to create a place where folks could find God without feeling awkward throughout the entire experience. The result is Encounter, a brand new home-based cell church that meets in the Memphis area.

This church represents an innovative cell church structure that is a hybrid between cell church and a house church network. Pitman describes the church as a network of home-based *ecclesias*. Each of these churches has men's and women's cells. The idea is for the home-based units to be simple churches—or house churches who assemble on Sunday—and the gender groups to function as cells.

---

## Family Life Church

Cabot, AR
Pastor Dave Smith, Nazarene
**Facts:** 12 cells, 250 worship attendance
www.cabotfamilylife.org

Before this Nazarene church officially started, the leaders immersed themselves in cell church literature to clearly see what they wanted to eventually become. God birthed the vision for cells in their hearts.

Pastor Dave Smith started the first pilot cell in 2001, and they have since continued the process of multiplication, while gathering the cells together each Sunday to celebrate.

Smith writes, "The cell philosophy has given us the context for making disciples who are making disciples. Our cell groups are being the church that Christ called us to be in our community. The vision for our cells is to connect with Christ, one another, and pre-believers. It's happening! Last fiscal year we baptized 34 new believers. This year our goal is for 70. Our cell leaders are winning people to Jesus, participating in their baptism and discipling them to become future cell leaders. It's so much fun for me to see the church in action. I grew up in a very traditional church looking for something more. Cell church is the N.T. body life I was looking for."

---

## Grace Christian Church

Howell, NJ
Pastor Jeff Barbieri, Independent Bible church
**Facts:** 11 cells, 100 worship attendance
www.njgrace.org

In 2003, Pastor Jeff Barbieri stepped outside of his box and started a cell-based church called Grace Christian Church. Barbieri writes, "Though I am new at pastoring this way, it feels so natural. In the traditional church I was trying to superimpose the biblical principles of edification, equipping, and evangelism on a structure that was at best neutral and at times hostile to these functions. But in a cell church the very model gives birth to and supports these biblical functions." God is giving Grace Christian Church new converts, and they are effectively discipling these converts through the cell structure.

---

## Living Hope Christian Assembly

Hamilton, ON, Canada
Pastor Bob Leach, affiliated with Ministers Fellowship International
**Facts:** 50 cells, 650 worship attendance
www.living-hope.org

Pastor Bob Leach was part of the drug culture of the '70s and was saved in Kabul, Afghanistan, while on his way to India. He, along with his wife, Joanne, began attending a local church in 1974 and were called to be senior pastors in 1985.

Living Hope is a cell-based church that is connected with the worldwide G12 movement. Leach's first introduction to the cell concept came from the International Charismatic Mission in Bogota, Colombia. The church's web site declares, "We at Living Hope believe in a life-giving God who, in the foundation of His creation, created cells. These natural cells are the foundation of life, growth, and health. In the spiritual world God is using the same principle to reproduce His spiritual life through His Church." Their passion is to win, consolidate, disciple, and send people into ministry.

The church has effectively reached the non-Christian community, and today 60% of those attending the church are from the unsaved and unchurched world.

---

## Neighborhood Alliance Church

Lacey, WA
Pastor Larry Peabody, CMA
**Facts:** 10 cells, 175 worship attendance
www.naclacey.org

Larry Peabody adopted the cell church strategy in 2000 and has been gently guiding his congregation toward growth ever since. Peabody understands that people's values don't change overnight, and he has prepared himself and his church for a long transition.

Peabody places great emphasis on careful training of the laity with the goal of developing cell leaders. God has also used the cells to reach out through relational evangelism.

With regard to coaching cell leaders, Peabody has modified the Groups of 12 concept so that the leaders receive more grassroots support.

Peabody is constantly trying to adapt the cell model in his church. He writes, "We are trying to include a *cell moment* in our celebration service at least a couple of times a month. Yesterday, we heard from a young woman who has just graduated from St. Martin's college. Her cell became her 'home away from home.'"

---

## New Community

Spokane, WA

Pastor Rob Fairbanks, Calvary Chapel

**Facts:** 35 cells, 500 worship attendance, 2 church plants

www.new-community.com

New Community is an affiliate of the Calvary Chapel movement, started by Chuck Smith in Costa Mesa, California. The web site says, "New Community's vision is to establish an urban small-group driven church which wholeheartedly loves and worships God, boldly proclaims the gospel of Jesus Christ and unconditionally loves all people, regardless of background."

While giving a seminar at New Community, I was impressed by the church's attempt to be culturally relevant to a postmodern membership while staying true to the cell values that form the base of the church. Fairbanks was an early adopter of cell ministry and has bridged the gap between contemporary ministry and cell quality. I like his balance.

He loves cell ministry and has carefully and persistently introduced a new generation of postmoderns to the cell church.

---

## New Hope Christian Fellowship

Chino, CA
Pastor Dave Scott, Free Methodist
**Facts:** 30 cells, 400 worship attendance
www.newhopecf.org

Pastor Dave Scott not only can clearly articulate the values of cell-based ministry (perhaps the best value/mission statements to define the cell church that I've seen), but he also lives those values to those around him. Scott is leading a growing cell church because he practices what he preaches.

Every week Scott plays basketball in the gym. He sweats with sinners. He helps coach little league sports and has even picked up the hobby of *radio control cars*. These activities have opened doors of relationships with unchurched people. He also leads a cell in his neighborhood.

His values and priorities speak loudly: "I want to exemplify what it means to be a friend of sinners and I want you, congregation, to do the same."

Scott has done a superb job of adapting a conventional staff to cell-based ministry.

---

## New Life Community Church

Chicago, IL
Pastor Mark Jobe, non-denominational
**Facts:** 125, cells, 2000 worship attendance, 8 satellite locations
www.newlifechicago.com

New Life began in 1987 as a resurrection of a small, dying inner-city church. Mark Jobe, son of missionary parents from Spain, arrived in December 1985 and began to emphasize home-cell-group ministry in 1991. It has since grown into a multi-cultural, multi-site, cell-based church that meets in eight satellite locations throughout the Chicago area.

The coaching structure follows social networks as opposed to geography. That is, when a group multiplies, it stays in the zone regardless of location. The zones are divided into women's groups, men's groups, married couples, youth, specialty groups and Spanish-speaking groups.

The church has a clear training track that begins with new believers and equips the members to minister through the cell structure.

---

## New Life Worship Center

Central, SC
Pastor Eric Thompson, Assemblies of God
**Facts:** 10 cells, 75 worship attendance
www.newlifetoday.net

Pastor Eric Thompson tried many programs to involve the church in discipleship and evangelism. Yet none of them had the success or fruit he desired. Through the hard knocks of ministry, God led him to adapt the church to the cell vision.

The cell groups at New Life meet weekly for the purpose of evangelism and discipleship while the leadership groups (G12) meet for coaching every other week. Thompson says, "We are working on getting our cell leaders and cells out into the community in order to get the community into our cells."

Because the church was still very young when they began their transition, they didn't experience many difficulties. Thompson says, "We are excited about the fruit and our future."

---

## Newmarket Alliance Church

Newmarket, ON, Canada
Pastor Ian Knight, CMA
**Facts:** 40 cells; 250 Sunday worship attendance, 2 church plants
www.nmk-biz.com/newmarketchurch

This church has remained on the cutting edge during the past decade. The church isn't afraid to risk and obey what God is revealing. In my book *Groups of Twelve* I mentioned this church because of the creative application in applying G12 principles.

The church recently restructured the leadership to eliminate the title "senior pastor" and shift the board of elders from a "board of directors" role so that the lead pastor (now called lead elder) and elders would be a team of overseers of the church.

The church also began to experiment with the integration of house churches and cell groups. The founding pastor, Dave Brandon, writes, "Essentially Newmarket Alliance Church is becoming a church of churches. We are attempting to transition the worship service into a corporate gathering of churches."

---

## Northlake Baptist Church

Longview, WA
Pastor Mark Schmutz, American Baptist
**Facts:** 28 cells, 400 worship attendance

Pastor Mark Schmutz came to the church in 1996 and prayed that God would give him a strategy. God burdened his heart with the cell vision, and in 1999, with about 300 people, the congregation started the transition to cell church.

Although the going was tough, they continued to reach out and multiply. The church has since added 100 people and has multiplied the first prototype cell to the current twenty-eight cell groups.

Schmutz meets with a different zone of cell leaders each Wednesday night and meets with the youth zone occasionally (in months that have five Wednesdays). The youth pastor meets with the youth zone each week.

I appreciated the steady growth in both cell and celebration that I witnessed in this church. Rather than abruptly changing a structure, Schmutz guided the church through value change among the members.

---

## Oshawa Community Church

Oshawa, ON, Canada
Pastor Frank Sexias, non-denominational
**Facts:** 30 cells, 350 worship attendance
www.occonline.info

I was impressed with the way this eleven-year-old church follows the tested cell principles and then adapts those principles to their reality. Sexias, for example, regularly visits the International Charismatic Mission in Bogota but does not follow the strict G12 model, opting rather to follow cell church principles and adapt the church based on a clear understanding of cell ministry.

Each of the coaches leads a cell group while coaching leaders under his or her care. Coaches can point out potential leaders that they are preparing for future multiplications. The church has a great training track that it has developed over time. This church is part of MFI (Ministers Fellowship International).

---

## Reality, a Post Modern Church of Christ

Burlington, KY
Pastor David Dummitt, First Church of Christ
**Facts:** 18 cells, 300 worship attendance, 1 church plant
www.realityonline.org

Started in 2000, this cell church plant is located in northern Kentucky and is primarily directed to postmoderns. They are using an adapted coaching structure to care for their cell leaders. Dummitt says, "I think the modified G12 is a great system for postmoderns in the U.S. context. Relationships are so valued. The modified G12 allows for long-term coaching relationships. Time is probably the most valuable commodity and that's why we didn't adopt the pure G12. Two meetings a week plus weekend worship was a bit overwhelming for our leaders."

Dummitt recently left Reality to plant a church in Brighton, Michigan, with the NewThing Network, a movement of reproducing cell churches helping people find their way back to God (www.newthing.org).

This church represents the new generation of cell based churches that is God is raising up across the land.

---

## Riverside Community Church

Nutley, NJ
Pastor Don Flynn, CMA
**Facts:** 7 cells, 140 worship attendance
www.rccmetrocma.org

Riverside Community Church has been in transition to the cell-group model since February 2003 when they began with a twelve-week cell bootcamp, designed to bring everyone onto the same page. Flynn recognizes the growing pains but also rejoices in the great learning experience. He writes, "The key is to be in it for the long haul, and we are. There is no plan B! Value change is a slow and tedious process, but true change does not come without it." The church's commitment to making it happen over the long haul is reflected in its recent hiring of Les and Twyla Brickman, leading researchers of the cell movement worldwide, to help them in their transition.

Encouragement along the way always helps. One cell leader wrote to Flynn, "If it had not been for the way God weaved into your heart a burning desire for a cell church, He never would have weaved into my heart the freedom that I now have—in this particular way. I truly believe that your devotion to Him set in motion my freedom."

---

## Royal Ridge Church of God

Scarborough, ME
Pastor Brian Wade, Church of God
**Facts:** 23 cells, 275 worship attendance
www.royalridge.org

Since 2002, Royal Ridge Church of God has been in transition to the cell church structure. Their guiding vision is crystal clear: "to see hundreds of cell groups meeting throughout the week all around southern Maine, all coming together on Sunday for a giant celebration."

Royal Ridge believes that cell groups are as much for evangelism as they are for fellowship and accountability and that each member of a cell group is a potential cell leader. Through cell ministry, the church encourages members to enter the leadership track and prepare to become cell leaders.

I like the balance of this church. It highlights both cell and celebration; it also follows an adapted G12 coaching structure because of its particular cultural realities.

---

## South Shore Community Church

Bridgewater, MA
Pastor Rob Reimer, CMA
**Facts:** 40 cells, 600 worshippers
www.southshorecommunitychurch.com

In 1994, founding pastor Rob Reimer began the first cell group with his wife and six others from the mother church. In October 1995, there were two cells with twenty-three people, and South Shore Community Church (SSCC) launched its first worship service. Cells have continued to multiply, people have trusted Christ, and the church has continued to grow.

Approximately 50% of the growth at SSCC comes through new converts. In fact, each cell has the rule that it must reach at least three people for Christ in order to multiply.

Reimer is very clear about their cell emphasis: "The cell group is the backbone of SSCC. The cell group features praying for each others' needs, discussing how to apply God's Word, developing authentic relationships, contributing to others' spiritual formation, and participating in a team effort to share the good news about God's love."

Each zone pastor at SSCC also leads a cell group, along with coaching other cell leaders. Reimer envisions the zone pastors working together in teams to more effectively care for the cell leaders under them.

## Touch Family Church

Houston, TX
Founding Pastor Ralph Neighbour, non-denominational
**Facts:** 16 cells, 175 worshippers
www.touchfamily.com

Ralph Neighbour and cell church are synonymous. In my seminars I'm fond of saying, "I believe that Ralph Neighbour is the premier world expert on cell church."

One key reason I respect Ralph so much is that he's a practitioner. He doesn't just write about cell church—he practices it. He founded Touch Family Church in Houston in 2000. This innovative church is reaching the multi-ethnic mix of Houston, composed of nine nationalities, and conducts cells and worship in English, Chinese, and Spanish.

The church has started a first-class Internet-based seminary to train students in cell ministry at www.touchglocal.com. Bill Beckham, worldwide expert on cell church, is now working with Neighbour as part of the pastoral team.

The web site says, "We are a cell church patterned after the New Testament model, focused on loving God and loving people and committed to the personal growth of every member." The vision of the TOUCH Family is to penetrate the 88% of Houstonians who are totally unchurched.

There are no "members" at this church—only "missionaries" along with the conversions made among the unreached. Baptisms are performed by all who bring unbelievers to faith, and the Lord's Supper is practiced in the cells. Those hearing the Word on Sunday morning sit around tables rather than in rows. The end of the message allows opportunity for each table to discuss the content of the message, and all ministry takes place through members ministering to one another. Web sites include: www.touchfamily.com; www.touchranch.com; www.liftgroups.com; www.coverthebible.com.

---

## Valley Church

North Vancouver, BC, Canada
Pastor Owen Scott, Full Gospel
**Facts:** 42 cells, 600 worshippers
www.valleychurch.ca

When Owen and Val Scott started pastoring Valley Church in 1986, it already had a thirty-one-year history but only twenty-two members. Since that time, God has done exciting things, molding a church that is both multi-racial and inter-generational. And this church gives all glory to God, depending on prayer to make the growth happen. In the fall of 2000, Valley Church leadership decided to move the congregation toward becoming a cell church. Matthew and Winnie Low, who had extensive experience and training in cell ministry, were brought on staff in 2001 to help implement the cell model at Valley Church.

I was very impressed with the bold value statements that this church proclaims:

- The cell is the center of the church.
- The cell is the center of ministry in the church.
- The cell is the church and meets every week.
- The cell is the place of edification (building up), it's not a Bible study per se.
- The cell is the community of accountability and encouragement.
- The cell members are to reach out to their pre-believing friends and loved ones (*oikos*).
- The cells gather together with other cells weekly to celebrate Christ.
- The cell multiplies itself as a mark of a healthy cell and a healthy church.

This church has done an excellent job of using Alpha to reach non-Christians while carefully integrating this ministry within the cell structure.

---

## Victory Christian Center

Tulsa, OK

Pastor Billy Joe Daugherty, non-denominational

**Facts:** 900 cells, 8670 weekend service attendance, and 184 international Bible schools in 52 countries

www.victorytulsa.org

Victory Christian Center, founded and led by Billy Joe Daugherty, is an exciting cell church, one of the largest in North America. This church has been on a journey since the early 1980s. Initially inflamed with the cell vision through Cho's church, Victory has been adapting ever since. As I talked with people during and after my first seminar at Victory, I was impressed with the various cell qualities in the church.

First, Daugherty is clearly leading the charge. He has the excellent help of a cell champion in Jerry Popenhagen, but the vision for cell ministry comes from the top. Second, the church has a superb training track. People are set free to serve through their training track, and they understand that holiness will bring forth the best fruit. Third, they are following principles in their coaching structure, having adapted the G12 care structure to fit their own particular needs. They didn't blindly adopt the entire G12 care structure, but rather they adapted it to fit their own situation. Fourth, every cell receives the cell lesson in the weekly bulletin and is encouraged to follow the five-fold purposes of the cell.

The best thing about Victory is that they are passionate about reaching lost souls for Jesus Christ.

___

## Wenatchee Free Methodist Church

Wenatchee, WA
Pastor John Paul Clark, Free Methodist
**Facts:** 100 cells, 1000 worship attendance
www.wenfmc.org

This church has been an important witness in the community for more than 100 years. Clark came in 1996 and has since been integrating the church into cell ministry. He has led and multiplied cell groups, and he understands cell values. Their web site mission statement declares, "At WFMC we're passionate about loving God, loving each other, and loving those who do not yet know Jesus. Each of these purposes is best lived out in a small group—a small community of between five and fifteen people where 'life' is shared."

When I held a seminar in this church I sensed a great excitement for what God is doing through cell ministry. A lot of this can be attributed to Floyd Schwanz, the cell champion.[10] Schwanz wrote the excellent book, *Growing Small Groups*.[11] Before joining WFMC, he was a key cell pastor at Dale Galloway's church in Portland, Oregon. Schwanz's fire for cell ministry is contagious, and his ministry stokes the flame of cell ministry for everyone in the church.

## Wesleyan Fellowship

Atlanta, GA

Pastor Tom Tanner, Weslyan

**Facts:** 74 cells, 900 worship attendance

www.wesleyanfellowship.org

I first met the pastor and staff of Wesleyan Fellowship in a seminar in Atlanta in 1999. It was the same year that this church decided to dedicate itself to become a cell-based church. Tanner writes, "We are still figuring out some things, but we are having fun and God is most definitely blessing us as well as changing us." I love this church because it's such a great example of following the principles while adapting each step of the way.

This church, like all churches on this list, hasn't arrived. Yet they are committed to a New Testament style of ministry that emphasizes transformation through a careful disciplemaking process.[12]

## Western Branch Community Church

Chesapeake, VA

Pastor Jim Wall, Pentecostal Free Will Baptist

**Facts:** 76 cells, 1500 worship attendance, 4 church plants

www.wbcc.net

Pastor Jim Wall, a former missionary to the Philippines for nine years, felt led to return to the U.S. in 1989 and plant a church committed to reaching people who still believed in God but had given up on the church.

In 1996, he began to move the church toward cell-based ministry, mainly because of the "hundreds of baby Christians crying for nourishment and no one to feed them!"

The Sunday morning services are very evangelistic. They are not purely "seeker," but they do provide a very accepting environment and they work to ensure that the songs and messages are understandable to the average unchurched person. The members create a warm, accepting atmosphere and are trained to be focused on meeting newcomers and ministering to hurting people. The members are challenged not to spend their Sunday morning time with each other. Their Sunday evening services are more oriented toward the mature believer.

Wall writes, "Today, we are operating under a hybrid 5x5/G12 model. As a result, we have effectively closed our back door (only a trickle now) and newcomers who choose to stay with us flow right into cell life. More importantly, we are watching new believers come to Christ every week *and* members grow up in Christ!" Wall also coaches the leaders through a monthly huddle in which the leaders receive vision casting, prayer for their needs, and ongoing leadership training.

## York Alliance Church

York, PA

Pastor David King, CMA

**Facts:** 20 cells, 500 worshippers

In 1998, key leaders from York Alliance went to an ACTS cell seminar in Virginia and became convinced that God wanted them to become a cell-based church. Starting with three pilot small groups made up of board leaders and members, the church has been on a journey ever since. Transforming an eighty-year-old church is not an easy task, as the pastors know only too well. From 1998 until now, God has been molding King and the staff to live the values they expect the rest of the church to follow.

The journey has also been an exciting one. This church has testimony after testimony of transformed lives through cell ministry. As I interviewed cell leader after cell leader, my own life was transformed by the total dedication to friendship evangelism that many of the groups are experiencing. God is molding this church with a passion for the lost through small group evangelism.

Cell church is a great way to do ministry—even in North America. It works among people in a wide range of denominational and non-denominational backgrounds. The churches described here demonstrate that the cell church strategy can be implemented throughout North America.

As in most of life's endeavors, success is not pain free. Becoming a cell church requires counting the cost, planning carefully, preparing the church through prayer and preaching, and especially involving the top leadership. Unless the lead pastor and key leaders model what they want others to follow, the church will go nowhere fast.

Remember also that weak, human pastors—just like you and me—shepherd North American cell churches. And these cell churches are composed of normal, hurting people. Their cells perform the function of hospital care and delivery rooms, spreading out over the city to reach and care for the sick and dying.

The beauty and power of cell ministry is in its fulfillment of the very words of Christ, "For the Son of Man came to seek and to save what was lost" (Luke 19:10).†

---

† I will provide up-to-date statistics of the North American cell churches included in this chapter at **www.cellchurchsolutions.com/articles/worldwide/NorthAmerica. htm**

# Section Two

**What It Will Take to Make Cell Church Work
in North America**

## Chapter Six

# Back to the Basics

**T**he chapters in this section of the book embody the principles necessary to make cell church work in the North American context. I specifically chose the following principles because of their unique application to North America. I believe the following chapters highlight the principles that North American leaders and churches need in order to succeed in cell ministry. These principles represent the mindset shifts that a pastor and congregation need to make to successfully chart the waters of cell church ministry in North America and beyond.

## The total solution

In 2004 we discovered termites in our Moreno Valley house. They appeared near the garage door and on the posts in our backyard. We invited several insect specialists to examine the damage. The major questions these specialists had to answer were

1. How far had the termites penetrated?

2. Was a total solution or a partial solution needed (i.e., did they need to cover the entire house or was it sufficient to spray only particular parts of the house)?

Some specialists suggested the total solution; others recommended a partial fix.

The North American church has limped along with a partial solution for too long. Church-growth experts have suggested a variety of solutions, but the termites keep coming back. The world's agenda in North America is just too alluring. Luxury and the pursuit of pleasure dominate the media; the Sunday jolt—even with great preaching—is the partial solution.

We need God's renewal and revival.

## Power ahead of techniques

"Joel, remember to tell pastors that commitment to prayer is the main thing," my wife Celyce reminds me. Celyce knows from experience that prayer power drives successful cell churches. She also knows that I can easily forget this truth and start overemphasizing the technical side of cell church ministry.

I reread a famous church-growth book that mentioned prayer only in passing while spending 100 pages on how to attract a crowd. "There's something wrong with this," I thought. "If we can attract the seeker by singing fewer songs, using less Scripture, and making it more comfortable, who is in charge? Jesus Christ? Human techniques?"

---

*I believe that those who will even consider church in today's
postmodern society will most likely come because they are
drawn to Jesus—not to human techniques.*

---

I believe that those who will even consider church in today's postmodern society will most likely come because they are drawn to Jesus—not to human techniques. The most powerful witness to non-believers in a postmodern age is demonstrating the power of God, whether in the cell or celebration. People in today's society go to a cell or celebration because they want to see Jesus.

A pastor can grow a church numerically without prayer. But it will be a weak church that lacks power. Transformed lives will be the exception rather than the norm.

How much better to build a church that breathes New Testament life from every pore—where people can feel the power of the Spirit and sense that the church has been laboring on its knees. People come to Christ and sign up for cell ministry because of the Spirit's compulsion. God wants our churches to breathe this type of New Testament life. Prayer is the key to making this a reality.

Many churches feel little need for prayer because the programs and techniques are so effective. As long as the worship team performs, the pastor preaches a relevant message, and the administration flows without a hitch, everyone feels satisfied. As you examine these churches, however, you'll notice a fatal flaw: the lack of transformed lives. There is no power. Even God seems scheduled on the church calendar.

The first and foremost solution to the transformation of the church in North America is prayer—a humble, radical crying out to God for help. Commitment to prayer obliterates pride and forces us to rely solely on God Himself. It teaches us to depend on Him before looking at strategies—even cell ministry. The time has come to go beyond past remedies and fixes. We need a major overhaul, a total solution.

The Pentecostal/charismatic camp might be the fastest-growing segment of Christianity today, but it doesn't—or least shouldn't—have a corner on prayer. Commitment to prayer is the arsenal that God has given to His entire body. And it's the most important weapon God has given the Church to win souls and make disciples.

Churches—charismatic or not—that prioritize prayer realize that only God can give the growth. They realize that human techniques might work for awhile, but those techniques won't solve North America's core problem. God is clear about the fact that unless He builds the house, the laborers do so in vain.

Because cell church ministry flies in the face of Sunday-in, Sunday-out, it works best among a group of people committed to God's supernatural power that comes through prayer. Only through prayer can the church break down cultural resistance and live New Testament life styles in community with one another. Only through prayer and an emphasis on spirituality will members be willing to dedicate volunteer time to serve as cell leaders.

## Churches that pray

At Wellspring, the cell church I'm planting in Moreno Valley, California, we decided to practice this principle from the very beginning. We haven't arrived—in fact, we've just started—but we have begun on our knees. We have two prayer meetings per week, along with weekly cells, training, and coaching. We pray on Wednesday night and then dedicate another hour to prayer on Sunday night. I also encourage each cell to pray for one hour before the cell begins. None of us has extra time to pray, but we've decided to make prayer a core value of our church from the very beginning.

Cypress Creek Church in Wimberley, Texas, also prioritized prayer from its initial roots. Rob Campbell, the founding pastor, not only exemplified prayer but hired Cecilia Belvin, the pastor of prayer, as the first staff person. Today Cypress Creek Church has one of the most vital prayer ministries I have ever seen. God has blessed this church abundantly because they've placed Him first.

Prayer is cell church oxygen. To breathe normally, a church must be permeated with prayer. It doesn't matter whether a pastor is starting a cell church or is in transition to the cell church strategy, prayer has to be the first step.

## Prayer in the cell group

Prayer dependence should be seen in the cell as well as in the larger body—not just one or the other. Cell prayer and church-wide prayer provide the one-two punch to the cell driven church. Prayer can't be over-emphasized, in my opinion. Some great ideas to jump start cells for prayer include the following:

- Break into groups of two or three. This allows more people to enter into prayer and is less intimidating for quieter members.
- Ask individual cell members to intercede, calling on them by name.
- Train your group to pray short, conversational prayers that provide greater interaction and agreement. This allows more people to pray and helps prevent one person from dominating.
- During the last fifteen minutes of the cell, ask the men to go into one room to pray and the women to pray in another room. Often there is more liberty to freely share prayer requests among gender-specific groups.

Cells are simply the conduit of the Holy Spirit; they are not an end in themselves. Prayer empowers cells and makes them a blessing to others.

## Prayer power in North America

North America desperately needs God's moving to break down walls of secular unbelief. Churches across the land need to remember that the battle is spiritual. Satan and his demonic hordes laugh at powerless, prayerless churches. These same dark forces become extremely worried, however, when churches pay the price through prayer.

Prayer, along with worship, fills a church with God's presence and power. Non-Christians are converted when they experience God's power because God created them for Himself, and hearts will remain restless until finding rest in Him alone. Prayer power creates the atmosphere for these same non-Christians to "fall down and worship God, exclaiming, 'God is really among you' " (1 Cor. 14:25).

The cell church is uniquely capable of raising an army of warriors who go forth in God's power, penetrating a lost world for Jesus. When this happens through churches on their knees, a new day will dawn for North America. The best is yet to come.

## Chapter Seven

# Life-giving Communities

**J**im and Cathy live in a suburb of a major city. Jim wakes up early, buys coffee at Starbucks, and then fights traffic for an hour to arrive at work. Jim eats lunch alone in a fast-food restaurant close to his job. During evenings and weekends, Jim is too exhausted from the long commute to interact with friends and family. He doesn't know his neighbors and has little time for community or school involvement.

He barely has time for Cathy or his children. Jim feels increasingly isolated from his family, co-workers, and neighbors. He wonders if his life has meaning or a larger vision or purpose.

In many parts of the world, the need for relationships is not as urgent as it is in North America. In those areas, family is prioritized above all else. In North America, relationships are often ignored. Things and money are more important. Getting ahead takes precedence over people.

The cell emphasis of community is a principle that is absolutely essential in North America. Community through cell life might be the most attractive aspect of cell ministry to transform Christians and reach those who don't know Jesus.

## The need for community

The current generation is paying the social price for valuing job success over family wholeness. Fifty percent of the children in North America today come from broken homes. Many in this post-Christian era are earnestly longing for familial relationships. They've suffered at the careers of their parents and the fast-paced cultural norm of this society.[1]

Harvard professor Robert Putman, in his book *Bowling Alone*, describes the downward decline of social relationship from post-World War II until the present. Statistically, Putnam pinpoints the lack of community among North

Americans because of increased television watching, flight to the suburbs, long-distance travel to work, and generational change.[2]

The neglect of social relationships has caused a tremendous void in North America today and a new hunger for community. Generation Next is a postmodern people who are struggling and searching for a sense of belonging and connectedness. They want

- to experience community and deeper relationships
- to believe that life is meaningful and has a purpose
- to be appreciated and respected
- to be listened to and heard

The cell group offers face-to-face interaction. It gives each member the chance to receive a listening ear, gentle encouragement, and a warm embrace. Instead of being the 278th and 279th people on the Sunday morning roll, people like Jim and Cathy have a name, a reality, a life.

## The nature of cell

Cells, unlike large-group celebration, connect people in face-to-face gatherings. No one can sit in the back seat; everyone is in the front row.

In the cell, each member is a priest who ministers. The members minister to one another and fulfill Paul's encouragement to the believers in the first-century church, "I myself am convinced, my brothers, that you yourselves are full of goodness, complete in knowledge and competent to instruct one another" (Rom. 15:14).

Cell ministry is specifically designed to tear away the layers of pain and the hidden agendas and to apply God's inerrant Word to real needs. Great cell leaders allow people to apply the biblical passages to circumstances of daily life.

A cell meeting will often include four Ws: welcome, worship, the Word, and witness (or works). All four of these elements help the cell develop community. The icebreaker (welcome) touches some area of the past, and, though often humorous, it reveals a lot about the person. Then worship draws the members into the presence of the living God. The cell lessons (the Word) avoid the impersonal, one-man-show mentality and ask each to contribute. Finally, the vision-casting time (witness) requires group involvement—working together to win a lost world to Christ.

For cells to maintain the ministry focus, they must remain small. Someone has said, "Community begins at three and ends at fifteen." Keeping the group small maintains the community feeling. Only in the intimacy of a small, closely knit group will people confess their faults one to another in order to be healed (James 5:16).[3] Open sharing becomes difficult when the group grows to more than fifteen.

The quest for community should stir each cell to develop new leaders in order to eventually multiply new groups that will offer fresh hope to people in need.

---

*Cell ministry is specifically designed to tear away the layers of pain and the hidden agendas and to apply God's inerrant Word to real needs.*

---

Some cell leaders insist on taking two to three hours in the actual cell meeting. People leave immediately afterward because of their busy schedules. I strongly recommend that a cell meeting end after one and a half hours to allow time for refreshments and spontaneous interaction. It's often during the refreshment time that the best sharing, evangelism, and community life take place.

Not all community or ministry happens in the cell group. Cells are often the springboard for one-on-one relationships that take place outside the meetings. Janet, a member of our cell, silently suffered in her marriage because of a total blackout of communication. She wisely didn't blurt out the hurt she carried (which would have maligned her husband to those in the group). She did, however, spend hours with my wife outside the cell meeting, receiving prayer and encouragement. God ministered to her in the small-group environment but healed her in the relationships that extended from the cell.\*

## The difficulties of promoting community

Promoting small-group ministry is not easy or popular. Denominational pressure often influences leaders to prioritize the Sunday event. (After all, that's what

---

\* My book *How to Lead a Great Cell Group Meeting* explains how to lead an exciting community-oriented cell group that practices the four Ws described above. See **www.cellchurchsolutions.com**, or call **1-888-344-CELL**.

gets counted in the denominational reports.) Many pastors feel the pressure to emphasize *anonymity* because they're told this is how to keep attendance high.

Most pastors have little time and energy left to build the cell infrastructure—to prepare God's people to do the work of the ministry. And many pastors frankly don't want to see the problems in their people. Pastor Frank said to me, "Joel, I didn't know I had so many dysfunctional people in my church until we started this small-group ministry. It's like I lifted up a wet log in a dark forest, only to see bugs scurrying everywhere."

Those same needy people had sat in Pastor Frank's church every Sunday with coats and ties, and outwardly everything seemed proper and in order. But as they began to interact with one another in the small-group environment, the needs, hurts, and disappointments surfaced.

Pastor Frank realized that his people needed to understand themselves before transformation could take place. He encouraged group members to share honestly to experience restoration, healing, and a sense of community.

The miracle that took place in Frank's church was because every member became a minister to help heal the hurts in others. Larry Crabb writes in his book *Connecting*, "Ordinary people have the power to change other people's lives. . . . The power is found in connection, that profound meeting when the truest part of one's soul meets the emptiest recesses in another's and finds something there, when life passes from one to the other."[4]

### Community and evangelism

One common objection is that if the small group is evangelizing, it won't grow in community. How can new people come into the group and the group still maintain a deep level of community? Research and experience show, however, that better, more biblical community develops when a cell reaches out to non-Christians. The newer person actually adds to the growth of the believers in the group by giving them an opportunity to minister—and thus grow.

When a small group has a common evangelistic objective, it starts working together to accomplish a goal. The common objective creates a unity and camaraderie. Everyone gets involved—from the person who invites the guests to the one who provides refreshments to the one who leads the discussion. The team plans, strategizes, and finds new contacts together.

The friendship and love (community) develops in the process of reaching out as a group to non-Christians. Today's broken society desperately needs a loving family. How will people find it unless small groups who are living in community are willing to spread it?

The cry of the lost drives cells to share their rich community rather than hoarding it among themselves. When multiplication takes place, new groups are available for lost people to receive wholeness.

## Community and transformation

To restore wholeness in a fractured society, God desires His twenty-first-century church to refocus on the priesthood of all believers—believers ministering to one another. This will happen in loving, small groups that encourage open, honest sharing. In this environment, churchgoers who get lost in the pews suddenly have a name and face. Church comes to life as people open up to one another.

I began this chapter with Jim's isolationism and loneliness. His need, along with the insistence of his wife, Cathy, stirred him to join one of the church's cell groups that met on Wednesday nights. The hardest part was walking through the door for the first time, but his fears were unfounded. He felt very comfortable, and the group didn't pressure him to talk. The next meeting was easier, and he even made a few friends. Within the first month, after hearing others transparently talk about their own needs, he felt comfortable enough to share personal prayer requests.

It's been one year now since Jim joined the cell group. His life has been transformed. His relationship with Cathy has also improved. He gets into his car for work each morning knowing he has a cell community with whom he can share his struggles. He realizes now more than ever that he needs fellow believers as he walks through the Christian life.

## Chapter Eight

# Group Evangelism

**B**ecause of the church growth we experienced during our eleven years of ministering in Ecuador, I spent time fine-tuning the cell system, the coaching structure, leadership development, and cell church details.

Just a few months after moving back to the United States in 2001, I flew to Sydney, Australia, to give a seminar at Liverpool Christian Centre. During the seminar, I shared the things on my heart, namely coaching structure, leadership development, and other details.

After the seminar, the associate pastor said, "I liked your seminar, Joel, but I want you to know that a lot of people came to this seminar to learn how to evangelize through cell groups. People in Australia are very individualistic, and they find it very hard to do cell evangelism in this western environment. I noticed that you didn't even talk about small-group evangelism."

I began to justify myself, trying to wiggle out of the conversation. God, however, clearly spoke to me through this associate pastor. I realized that I was not emphasizing small-group evangelism, almost assuming it would naturally happen as leaders were developed and trained. In Ecuador it did naturally happen, but in the western world, small-group evangelism is tough. It takes work. It needs to be prioritized.

Cell evangelism is the key distinguishing feature of cell groups—whether those cell groups are located in North America or other parts of the world. In receptive areas of the world (e.g., Latin America, Africa, Asia) the harvest flows through cell ministry. God's fresh revival makes it happen. Growth is not as easy, however, in North America and other western cultures. Cell evangelism, therefore, must be consciously promoted in North American cell groups on a regular basis.

## Penetrating

Many remember a time in North America when the Sunday evening church service was labeled "evangelism night." Many were won to Christ through those services. Few such services exist today. Most churches have discontinued the Sunday evening services for lack of attendance. The North American, post-Christian culture no longer feels obligated to go to church.

---

*Penetration means living as the community of the King where people live, work, and breathe.*

---

Now it's time for the church to *go to them*. The church must move from being the inviting church to becoming the invading church. Gibbs says, "It is commendable for the church to be 'seeker-sensitive' . . . but now, the church must itself become the seeker. More often than not, they [those being sought] will first need to be befriended by a Christian and linked to a small group of believers who can demonstrate the benefits and challenges of following Christ."[1]

Penetration means living as the community of the King where people live, work, and breathe. It means getting everyone involved in the process of penetrating a neighborhood, job site, or wherever the group is meeting.

## Fishing with nets

The group aspect of cell evangelism takes the burden off the leader and places it on everyone in the cell. It's net fishing as opposed to pole fishing. Pole fishing is done individually, while net fishing requires the help of many hands. Net fishing is a group effort and results in catching more fish, while fishing individually with a pole catches one fish at a time. When Jesus said to Simon and Andrew, "Come, follow me and I will make you fishers of men," He was talking about becoming net fisherman—that's the way they fished back then. The beauty of cell evangelism today is the casting out and drawing in as a result of the group effort.

For our cell group, this primarily meant regularly walking the streets to pray for people in the neighborhood. When we saw people outside, we greeted them in a friendly, loving way. Sometimes one of the members felt led to speak about Christ and invite the person to our cell.

Other group evangelism strategies include barbecues, picnics, friendship dinners (instead of the normal cell meeting order), evangelistic videos, special outreaches at Christmas and Easter, and placing an empty chair in the cell meeting and praying for someone to fill it.

One cell leader who attended my seminar near Portland, Oregon said, "Our cell group plans evangelistic outreaches every six weeks. We'll go to a Portland Trail Blazers basketball game or something else at least every six weeks. In this way, we're constantly reaching out and befriending non-Christians. The consistency prevents us from neglecting small-group evangelism."

The cell leader must remember that instead of doing everything himself—which will never create a feeling of community or develop new leaders—he should involve the team by

1. delegating the various parts of the weekly meetings to others and watch them learn as they do it
2. asking each member of the cell to pray over non-Christian contacts for several weeks before actually inviting the people to the cell group

Though group techniques abound, the primary emphasis should be on developing relationships with non-Christians with the goal of eventually inviting those non-Christians to the cell group.*

## Befriending sinners

Net fishing begins with each member of the cell getting to know non-Christians. Before conversion, there must be communication, which involves building relationships with non-Christians.

Jesus was a friend of sinners. The religious establishment, in fact, cast him out because he was always hanging out with sinners—those who needed him the most. McRaney says, "Postmodern people generally start farther away from Christ than their predecessors, and therefore will usually take longer in surrendering their life to Christ. So Christians will have to be intentional about

---

* www.cellchurchsolutions.com/articles/evangelism/sixKeys.htm talks about how to do cell evangelism. Find additional articles on cell evangelism at www.cellchurchsolutions.com.

developing relationships and planting seeds through servant and ministry evangelism projects."[2]

My family and I began developing relationships with our non-Christian neighbors in 2001. We didn't preach to them about Jesus right away, preferring to let them see our lives. The neighbors on one side accepted our invitation to come over for a barbecue. Several months later we invited them to our house to see a skit that my daughters performed.

We were disappointed when we invited them to our cell group and they turned us down, noting their crowded schedules on Sunday night. We made the same effort with the neighbors on the other side. We were not successful in getting them to come to our cell either.

The neighbor two doors down, however, did respond and started attending our cell. He was the divine appointment that God had been preparing. This particular neighbor loved the atmosphere in the small group because it provided a non-threatening place where he could talk and express himself. Cell evangelism works best when each of the members is proactively getting to know non-Christians and then inviting them to the cell.

## Being transparent

Cells provide a great atmosphere for non-Christians. Most cells, like our own, begin with food and an icebreaker. What was the first car you remember driving? and What was the first trophy you received? are examples of friendly icebreakers. We often have one of the children pick the icebreaker, and then the icebreakers are more down to earth: What is your favorite kind of donut? or Share what your favorite color is and then share why it is your favorite color.

After the icebreaker the facilitator starts the theme of the lesson—say, loneliness—usually taken from the pastor's Sunday morning message. The non-Christian is caught in the web of personal evangelism.

Transparency is the best evangelistic tool to reach non-Christians. People without Christ appreciate authenticity. They're thankful when Christians share struggles, because often the non-Christian is going through situations far worse but without Jesus to help. Cell evangelism is a very natural activity and penetrates the defenses of those who would never darken the door of a church building but need love and a sense of belonging.

## Positioning cells to evangelize

Evangelism starts in the cell, but the senior leader can help a lot by positioning the cells to evangelize.

Steve Fowler, pastor of East Hills Alliance Church in Kelso, Washington, guided the board and elders in the process of becoming a cell church over a period of several years. Fowler, understanding the evangelism DNA of the cell, positioned the life groups to reach non-Christians. In the church foyer, he placed a large bulletin board with pictures of each cell leader in a small fishing boat. The sign over the bulletin board declares "Life groups have gone fishin." Nets and fishing poles are portrayed in various graphics and wall hangings in the church. At East Hills, the life groups are fishing for souls. From the one prototype life group, the life groups have multiplied to fifteen.

---

*"...every church that tries to transition to the cell church strategy and fails, misses this key point of evangelism."*

---

Rob Reimer, founding pastor of South Shore Community Church in New England, is another great example of cell evangelism. Reimer says, "Something is unhealthy about cells that don't reach people. In my experience, every church that tries to transition to the cell church strategy and fails, misses this key point of evangelism. Some churches compromise this principle and multiply cells through transfer growth. It is an unforgivable cell church sin."

Rob Reimer doesn't want his cells to multiply unless they have reached new people for Christ. The cell members are instructed to get to know non-Christians, and they do that through a variety of means.[3] Above all, Reimer exemplifies the evangelism fervor he wants others to follow. He writes, "I'm passionate about reaching lost people, and I preach it and model it. If the senior pastor doesn't preach it, bleed it, and model it, people will listen to what he says, and do what he does! He has to lead the way."[4]

The lead pastor's role is critical in maintaining the evangelistic focus. The natural tendency is for groups to turn inward and become self-absorbing. Most churches have some variation of this type of group. To turn from inward to outward requires a lead pastor with a vision for cell evangelism.

## Harvesting through celebration

I believe that the purpose of a celebration service is primarily to focus on God and His glory. Non-Christians are evangelized by the powerful presence of God in the service. They will also be touched by the preaching of the Word. Many call this "worship evangelism," and it fits right in with the cell strategy.

Powerful, dynamic worship and expository preaching will best convert the sinner who comes to the celebration service. Gibbs says, "But in the heartfelt worship of a people surrendered to him, God is pleased to dwell in the praises of his people. Unbelievers are also likely to sense the presence of God. . . . Celebration evangelism is assuming a more prominent place, as distinct from the proclamation evangelism of the past."[5] Though I believe the cells should be the primary evangelism vehicle, many cell churches are very effective in reaping the harvest during the celebration service.

Crossroads United Methodist Church in Pittsburgh invites people to receive Jesus in nearly every service (normally by filling out a visitor's card). The Crossroads cell system is ready to preserve the fruit. The church works hard to make the celebration services both understandable to unchurched people and meaningful to believers.

Pastor Jim Wall of Western Branch Community Church in Chesapeake, Virginia, also draws in the harvest net every Sunday by speaking on themes that minister to unbelievers. The cells draw these new converts into cell life for spiritual growth and development.

## Persisting

Cell evangelism in the western world is about pressing on in the face of difficulties and obstacles. Emphasizing evangelism and refusing to be deterred by the lack of fruit isn't easy. It requires persistence and diligence. One pastor from England wrote saying, "One of the things that strikes me is that evangelism in Latin America and several other nations seems to be much easier through cells than here in England and in Europe." My response was simply one of encouragement, telling him to persist amid unbelief and resistance.

The reality is that church growth in general is much slower in North America. Rick Harrell, a pastor in Redlands, California, faced many depressing moments when adapting his ninety-year-old church to cell ministry. Cell evangelism didn't happen naturally. His cell leaders tried evangelizing and reaching out continually but saw little fruit. I constantly needed to encourage Harrell to press on through the dryness. As the months passed, his church began to see the fruit of cell evangelism and multiplication. But it wasn't easy.

God wants to do great things through cell ministry, but the key is persistence. Brock, one of the leaders under my care, faithfully invited non-Christians week after week. People said they would come but didn't show up. Brock persisted, although discouragement and doubt resided not far from the surface. What a joy it was when Brock came to my house one evening saying that two of his invitees had shown up on the same night.

I was reminded of the man who attended my cell seminar in Canada. During the seminar he raised his hand and said, "Joel, I appreciated what you said about persistence in cell evangelism. I work for a direct marketing company, and we're taught that every no we receive on the phone is just a step closer to a yes. How much more should we persist in the cause of winning lost men and women for Jesus Christ."

## Chapter Nine

# Disciple Making

**O**ne pastor bought into the cell church philosophy** but didn't change his inward value of church success. The value that success equaled Sunday attendance was deeply ingrained in his psyche.

As I coached him over the months, I found that he naturally spent more time trying to attract people to the Sunday celebration service. He focused on sermon preparation, visiting, and dreaming of a crowd on Sunday. Cell ministry received leftover attention. When I challenged him on this, he acknowledged that he got a high from the Sunday crowd and didn't get that same excitement from cell ministry.

This pastor was struggling with how to measure success. I began to coach him on viewing his success in terms of disciples made and sent out rather than in terms of attracting a large group on Sunday morning.

This chapter lays the philosophical framework for a change in mental attitude. The next two chapters on training and coaching give more practical solutions on how to practice the concepts in this chapter.

Redefining church-growth success in terms of making disciples rather than building attendance figures might be the most important shift in pastors' thinking to make cell ministry work in North America. It's not a matter of removing the success mentality from the North American mind. It's a matter of redefining what success really is.

## The reformation of church growth

I consulted the staff in one church that met weekly with the aim of planning for the Sunday service. All effort and activity were directed to making the Sunday event happen. They talked about the preparedness of the greeters, the excellence of the worship, the preciseness of the announcements, and the cleanliness of the restrooms. Their staff planning meeting shouted loudly that they had one goal in mind: attract and keep people in the Sunday worship.

Many leaders, like the ones I just described, take their cue from church-growth theory and believe that success equals more church members, which normally translates into how many are attending the celebration event on Sunday morning.

Successful cell church pastors, on the other hand, view success differently. They focus on how many pew sitters can be converted into disciples who will pastor home groups that will in turn evangelize and disciple others. The celebration is important, but celebration attendance is the result of the real work that takes place during the week.

The focus on cell infrastructure helps align the pastorate with the New Testament truth that the job of the pastor is to prepare God's people for works of service (Eph. 4:11–12).

This focus rescues the pastor from the role of star of the Sunday celebration (how can I make the celebration attractive enough to keep the people coming back?) to chief trainer and disciple maker (how can I prepare and release lay workers into the harvest by developing them to lead dynamic cell groups?).

Though both cell and celebration are important in the cell church, I believe the cell infrastructure should guide (or drive) the church.

Todd Hahn, minister to postmoderns, says, "The seeker/believer strategy was a God-send for the modern church, yet it may be meaningless for postmoderns. . . . Postmoderns are not interested in being attracted to a large service. They want to be prepared to serve. It's in the service that they themselves are set free. The next church needs to be ready to give and serve."[1]

The cell church strategy focuses on preparing laypeople to serve. It's guiding people from sitting in church to helping them go through a process of training, cell involvement, and cell leadership.

## The cell-driven church

The cell-driven church, in contrast to the Sunday-oriented model, focuses on the cell infrastructure. The pastor concentrates on growing the church from the inside out. Success equals turning members into ministers that lead cell groups.

Damian Williams grasped the cell-driven strategy. When Williams started pastoring Red Cedar Community Church in 2000, the church had 200 people attending on Sunday morning. He set the clear goal of making disciples that make disciples. He challenged everyone to get in the training track with the goal of eventually leading a cell group. He knew that not everyone would become a leader, but he believed that everyone could become one.

---

*The cell-driven strategy is straightforward and simple: concentrate on developing new leaders through multiplying cell groups, and they will in turn reap the harvest and pastor the church.*

---

Williams focused on leadership training to produce disciples. He concentrated on the cell infrastructure. He developed a core leadership team from among the successful cell leaders to coach the other leaders. For Williams, the hard work took place in the cell system and the result was Sunday morning attendance growth.

In spite of many obstacles and resistance, Williams pressed on with his vision to grow the church from the core to the crowd. In three and one-half years the cells grew to thirty and the cell attendance to 350. The infrastructure growth brought more than 500 to the Sunday celebration.

The cell-driven strategy is straightforward and simple: concentrate on developing new leaders through multiplying cell groups, and they will in turn reap the harvest and pastor the church. It's the strategy that Christ gave to His disciples in Matthew 9:37–38: "The harvest is plentiful but the workers are few. Ask the Lord of the harvest, therefore, to send out workers into his harvest field." The goal of new cells is the goal of new leaders being equipped and sent out as harvest workers.[2]

With this approach, a church can concentrate on multiplying the infrastructure—developing new leaders—and be assured of qualitative and quantitative growth. Outreach and evangelism are core values in this approach. A church that is constantly multiplying cells is penetrating the city with red-hot evangelistic fervor and diligent leadership development. Galloway wrote, "The concept is that first you build leaders. The leaders build groups. Out of these groups come more leaders and a multiplication into more groups."[3]

On a practical level, this means that the pastor of a cell-driven church will first dream, plan, and pastor the cell infrastructure. The first item of business, for example, in the team leadership meeting is cell ministry. Each team member will share about how his or her own cell is doing and then report on the health of the cells. After working through the cell ministry issues, the pastor will deal with celebration concerns—worship, announcements, and the cleanliness of the restrooms.

When the pastor is asked at a conference how many people are in his church, the cell-driven pastor will first talk about the number of cell groups, cell leaders in training, and attendance in the cells. Why? Because the pastor has a new definition of success.

## Incorrect application of the two-winged church

Bill Beckham coined the term "two-winged church" to refer to a cell church that focuses on both cell and celebration. Beckham taught that a two-winged church, one that emphasizes both cell and celebration, can fly much better than a church that only emphasizes one wing.

I agree with Beckham's terminology, but I've also noticed that some have misapplied this concept. I now recommend using the phrase "cell-driven church" because it gives a better sense of direction and purpose.

This became clear in one church, in which the pastor had delegated the celebration ministry to one pastor and the cell ministry to another. He was trying to balance both wings by delegating cell and celebration. The senior pastor tried to convince me that he was simply focusing on both wings. I noticed a total lack of integration among cells, celebration, and ministries.

In this particular church, the cell pastor was supposed to do the cell work and the celebration pastor was supposed to do the celebration work. The senior pastor simply tried to oversee both of them, hoping that the two-winged bird wouldn't nosedive into the ground.

With only one staff pastor overseeing cells, the rest of the team were free to pursue their own ministries, not directly related to cell ministry. When the staff came together, there was no cohesiveness or direction. Each staff person would report on his or her ministry.

The church pushed hard for church members to join the existing cells, yet the congregation resisted because the staff structure spoke loudly that cell ministry involved only one part of the church's program.

I counseled this church to start from the top. I told them to first move the staff through the transition, and the rest would be easy. Over and over I mentioned the cell-driven model rather than the two-winged approach so they could get a better picture of what they were trying to do.

This meant that the senior pastor had to lead the charge. He needed to wear the cell-director hat. I even encouraged the senior pastor to lead his own cell in order to gain experience and knowledge of cell ministry. I told him that he needed to be reading cell literature and staying in tune with cell ministry so he'd have something to give his staff members. "You can have a great cell structure like a model car," I told him, "but just like the car doesn't work without the engine, without the senior pastor's cell passion and guidance, the cell structure doesn't work."

I counseled each staff member to lead a cell and oversee a few of the existing cell groups. Coaching cells would be their primary pastoral identity. Each would also have his or her ministry (e.g., worship, training, C.E., etc.) but the primary identity would be that of cell pastor.

I counseled them to talk about the cells first in their staff meetings. To do this effectively, each staff member would need up-to-date statistics on the state of the cell ministry. During this time, the staff could plan, pray, and envision new disciples. I told them to afterward discuss ministry items such as ushers, worship, preaching, and training.

I kept coming back to the idea of the cell-driven church. I had to help the pastor overcome his faulty vision of the two-winged church. I told him that the church needed to judge success by how well it was able to grow the infrastructure.

This example is a practical illustration of how the cell-driven church works. Each team member—whether staff or volunteer—is primarily responsible to care for the cell groups. The senior leader and staff are intimately involved in cell ministry—in most cases even leading a cell group. The first item of business in the staff meeting is a detailed account of the cells that met during the week.

Success is measured in a practical way. It works its way into the staff meeting, the announcements (see Chapter 13), and even the pastor's preaching schedule. The cell-driven senior pastor is not hesitant to allow others to share the pulpit, because he knows that his chief role is to be head coach of the cells. Several of the senior pastors I'm working with, in fact, preach only sixty percent of the time, allowing others to preach and develop their gifts and talents.

*The cell-driven senior pastor is not hesitant to allow others to share the pulpit, because he knows that his chief role is to be head coach of the cells.*

## Disciple defined

If the cell-driven strategy redefines success for a church, it's important to understand the end product of that success. Jesus made that clear in Matthew 28:18–20 when He told His disciples to make new disciples.

But what is a disciple? CrossPoint Community Church (CCC) wrestled with this question. CCC's mission statement says their goal is to make disciples who make disciples, but the church had to go one step farther and define what a disciple is.

Because I'm involved in coaching this church, we wrestled together with questions about the definition of discipleship. Pastor Jim Corley and I both agreed that a disciple is a follower of Christ, but we needed to know how that would look in practical terms. Corley and his key leaders were uncomfortable with the idea that a disciple equals a cell leader.

God gave wisdom to break down how a disciple could be defined in the cell church paradigm at CCC. I recommended that the church define a disciple in the following way:

- **D-1 Disciple** (member of a cell and training track)
  The first step is that a person attending CCC is in a cell and the training track (see Chapter 10). It's in this process that the person is baptized and taught to obey all the things that Christ has commanded (Matt. 28:18–20). Key steps in the training process include doctrinal teaching, holiness, baptism, evangelism, and preparation to minister to others.

- **D-2 Disciple** (associate leader)

  The next step is that the disciple lives out in practice what he or she is learning. The term D-2 disciple defines a person who is in a cell, taking the next step in the training track, and actually helping in cell leadership. Such a person is playing a significant role in the cell group and is consciously preparing to facilitate his or her own cell group.

- **D-3 Disciple** (cell leader)

  The next step is gathering people together and leading a cell group. The disciple has gathered friends and family and is facilitating the cell group. He or she has graduated from the training track.

- **D-4 Disciple** (multiplication leader)

  This is when the cell leader has developed another disciple who has multiplied out and is leading his or her own cell group (has gone through the D-1 to D-3 process). I would call a multiplication leader a D-4 disciple.

Because the cell-driven strategy grows from the core to the crowd, it's essential to have a clear picture of the desired goal. While acknowledging that the primary goal of the Christian life is to become like Jesus, it's essential to define this in practical terms within the church framework. The D-1 to D-4 understanding of discipleship helps guide a believer through a clearly defined equipping process.

From a practical standpoint, the goal is to make disciples, and the cell-driven strategy makes that happen by asking all members to go through a training track that prepares them to become disciples who minister to others.

## Cells as disciple makers

People often ask me why I believe in cells so much. "Well," I tell them, "I don't believe in cells. I believe in raising up new leaders. I believe in disciple making." My commitment to cell ministry is really a commitment to leadership development.

Cells are simply the best vehicle for developing leaders—they're leader breeders. Programs and tasks in the church, in contrast, don't develop and release leaders. Leaders are certainly not developed and released by sitting in church on Sunday morning or worshipping in a large group. I believe they are developed in a cell environment, where everyone is able to exercise spiritual gifts and influence others.

In a group of three to fifteen people who meet weekly outside the church building for the purpose of evangelism, community, and discipleship with the goal of multiplication, a person has the perfect atmosphere to become like Jesus Christ and to learn how to minister to others.

There's no end to the possibilities when discipleship becomes a way of life. The cell church majors in this. Such development simply doesn't happen very often in a choir group, usher group, Sunday school class, or board meeting. Potential cell leaders are best developed in holistic groups that emphasize evangelism, community, discipleship, and multiplication.

Some think that only certain people are talented enough to facilitate a cell group or that a person needs a particular gift to lead a cell group. My book *Home Cell Group Explosion* exposes this fallacy, showing through research from a statistical study of 700 cell leaders in eight countries that anyone can facilitate and successfully multiply a cell group. I believe, in fact, that facilitating a cell group is part of the process of maturing and becoming more like Jesus. When a person ministers to others, that same person receives much more and discovers God in new and exciting ways.*

## Biblical and doable success

Measuring success by developing disciples who make disciples is biblical and doable. One Australian engineer who became a cell church pastor wrote to me saying, "Joel, judging our performance by Sunday numbers is dangerous both ways. A good Sunday makes us think we're doing okay (when we may not be) and a bad Sunday . . . well you know what that can do to us pastors. But why judge ourselves by something we have no control over?"

I believe the result of making disciples who make disciples will be Sunday attendance growth, but it's the result rather than the major focus.[4] The Lord will give the Sunday morning increase in the process of making disciples who make

---

* *Home Cell Explosion* is available at **www.cellchurchsolutions.com** or by calling **1-888-344-CELL**.

disciples. A new excitement and liberation will take place as people are sent out as workers in the harvest.†

## Relief in celebration

Much of the debate today between postmodern worship (more experiential and worship oriented) and modern worship (less worship oriented and more seeker sensitive) misses the key point about making disciples through cell ministry. The goal in both postmodern and modern worship seems to be on attracting a crowd to the worship service.

---

*When churches begin practicing the cell-driven model,*
*the result is a true celebratory feeling on Sunday morning....*
*People can freely worship the living God and find Him.*

---

While the cell-driven model *normally* emphasizes worshipping and experiencing God in the celebration service, the cell-driven model puts its primary effort into building the infrastructure that in turn grows the worship service.[5]

Cell members do need the celebration time to hear God's inerrant Word from a prepared pastor/teacher, understand the overall vision and direction from the pastor, and worship the living God, but they also need to apply that teaching in the small-group atmosphere.[6]

When churches begin practicing the cell-driven model, the result is a true celebratory feeling on Sunday morning. The anxious feeling of trying to impress the seeker or to perform is lifted in the cell church. People can freely worship the living God and find Him.

## The end in view

One pastor shared an illustration of planting tomatoes versus planting a coconut tree. The tomato plant grows quickly and provides immediate results, but it dies at the end of one year and needs to be replaced. The coconut tree, on the other

---

† **www.cellchurchsolutions.com/articles/churchLeaders/howToSetGoals.htm** talks about the specifics of setting goals in the cell church.

hand, grows more slowly and bears fruit later, but it lasts for a lifetime. "I want to plant a coconut tree," the pastor said. "I want to prepare myself and my church for long-term success in small-group ministry." I encourage leaders to opt for the coconut tree style of small-group ministry.

Making disciples who make disciples is the key to long-term success. When a pastor believes that the cell-driven strategy is the key to long-term success, he will start building the cell infrastructure and make it his chief priority. This new mindset will affect everything he does and eventually everything the church does. The ultimate goal is obeying Jesus Christ, who gave clear orders to His church.

## Chapter Ten

# Doable Training

**" Whena** **hen you spoke on the training track,** it all made sense,"
one pastor told me. He had sat through all of my PowerPoint
presentations about the definition of a cell, multiplication, cell church history,
cell church principles, and even how to make the transition. The training track,
however, was the vital ingredient that made everything clear.

I had been coaching this pastor for several months, but his traditional view
of church education hindered him from understanding how to rapidly develop
harvest workers through specific training. This pastor, like so many other North
American pastors, was accustomed to promoting general Christian education on
Sunday. It suddenly dawned on him that there was a major difference between
education and training.

Education never ends. Training, on the other hand, touches specific skills
and lasts a limited time. Neil F. McBride, a Christian educator who has written
extensively about small groups, says, "Education is an expanding activity;
starting with where a person is at, it provides concepts and information for
developing broader perspectives and the foundations for making future analysis
and decisions. On the other hand, training is a narrowing activity; given whatever
a person's present abilities are, it attempts to provide specific skills and the
necessary understanding to apply those skills. The focus is on accomplishing a
specific task or job."[1]

McBride's insight about training being a *narrowing activity* versus the
*lifetime process* of education touches the nerve of cell leadership training.
Understanding specific training that leads to a person's becoming a cell
facilitator (disciple) is paramount in making the cell church work in North
America. It will require a new attitude about how to develop and release
disciples.

## Rapid preparation of disciples

The training track is a clearly defined path that prepares believers to become disciples who are leading cell groups. Synonyms for the word "track" include path, route, channel, and road. An equipping track takes the new believer from point A to point B. The training is specific, and the end result produces disciples who are leading cell groups.

Cell church training tracks feature clarity of training. They are not fuzzy. The key word that defines the best equipping tracks is the word "doable." It entails a definite beginning and ending. It means that a new person entering the church can readily understand the system—what it takes to go from A to B.

In the previous chapter I talked about a D-1 disciple as someone who is in a cell and in the training track. The person learns basic doctrine in this step and the action step is baptism. I then identified a D-2 disciple as one who is participating in the cell and living out what he or she is learning in the training. A D-3 disciple is someone who has completed the training track and is leading a cell group. A D-4 disciple is someone who has multiplied the cell and has been invited to participate in higher-level training.

Disciples are developed at each level of the journey, from conversion to leading a cell group—and then beyond leading a cell group to further training.

## Differences from general education model

The conventional Sunday model of church emphasizes Christian education on Sunday. The emphasis is biblical information for those taking Sunday school classes.

Though the intentions are excellent, most believers go away full of knowledge but with little practical outlet to practice that knowledge. Far too often the knowledge fails to produce practical results. Disciples are lost along the way and there is no clear way of tracking whether the knowledge acquired has made an impact.

Getting lost in the educational machinery is a recurring flaw in the general education approach to leadership training. Education lasts for a lifetime; training is for a specific purpose. The church should encourage members to be lifetime learners, but it also must train the members to specifically become harvest workers.

## Principles

Cell church training needs to be *doable* with regard to time and *flexible* with regard to options in taking it. Flexibility happens when church leaders understand the key principles common in all the best training tracks around the world and then adapt those principles to their own contexts. Seven key principles are vital to effective training tracks.

### Principle #1: Keep the training track simple

Many churches fall into the trap of over-complicating the first level of training. They try to place too many steps in the first level, making the training track long and cumbersome. Potential small-group leaders never arrive at the point of actually leading a group.

Don't over complicate the initial training track that makes disciples of new believers and prepares them to reach out to friends and neighbors through cell ministry. Most cell church equipping tracks prepare their leaders in the following areas:

- basic doctrine
- freedom from bondage (encounter retreat)
- personal devotions/quiet time
- personal evangelism
- leadership training

### Principle #2: Provide action steps with the training

The best training is accompanied with practical, on-the-job experience. The potential leader needs to see and experience community life, especially evangelism. In the training track that I'm developing, I encourage the following action steps:

- **First step:** learn foundational truths of the Christian life.
  **Action step:** get baptized.

- **Second step:** attend an encounter retreat .
  **Action step:** break from sinful habits.

- **Third step:** learn how to have a quiet time.
  **Action step:** have a daily quiet time .

- **Fourth step:** learn how to evangelize.
  **Action step:** befriend non-Christians and share the gospel message.
- **Fifth step:** learn how to lead a cell group.
  **Action step:** start and lead a cell group.

When I started training the potential leaders at Wellspring, I noticed that on the evangelism step, they pled with me to show them how to do it. They wanted to see a practical example of evangelism. We went on prayer walks together, praying for the neighborhood. God gave us opportunity to share our faith and reach out to people around us.

The same was true with the manual on how to lead a cell group. The trainees wanted to practically experience what they were learning, knowing they would soon be practicing those same principles in their own cell groups.

### Principle #3: Prepare a second level of training for small-group leaders

My advice is to divide your training into at least two levels. The first level should include the five basic areas or steps mentioned above (each area is normally embodied in a manual).

The second level should include additional doctrinal courses, a spiritual warfare course, teaching on spiritual gifts, etc. There is a lot of room for creativity, and many excellent courses and materials are available. One cell church decided to use their denomination's theological education by extension training for this second level.

Cell leaders deserve special treatment because of their important, foundational role in the church. Offer them all the help and training that they need in order to be effective.

Some cell churches even offer a third and fourth level of training, all the way to pastoral ministry. Faith Community Baptist Church features an extensive training program to prepare higher-level leaders. Bethany World Prayer Center hosts a three-year Bible school on its property. Neither church requires higher education for all cell leadership—it's simply provided for those who feel called to full-time ministry (and who have been successful in leading and multiplying their cell groups).

### Principle #4: Acknowledge variety in methodology

Some people believe that the only way to train new believers is one on one. Others disagree and train new believers in a group setting. Don't confuse the training methodology (where or how you train people) with the training track.

I've noticed a great variety of methodologies for implementing the training (e.g., one-on-one discipleship, one-on-two or -three, training after the cell group meeting, training during Sunday school hour, seminars, retreats, or a combination of all of them). I suggest teaching the training track during the Sunday school hour, which is often connected to the worship service. Then I suggest that those who can't attend during that time slot be given the freedom to take the same training before the cell starts, after the cell finishes, during a day-long training in a home or be given other options to complete the training.[2]

### Principle #5: Use only one equipping track

Though flexibility should be allowed in the choice of training methodology, I counsel churches to have only one training track—although that one training track can be adapted to age specific groups.

After deciding on a church-wide training track (ideally both first and second levels), a church should require that all future leaders pass through the same training. Mature leaders who have taken lots of training in the past could be given credit for subjects they've already mastered (e.g., Bible doctrine, evangelism, how to have a quiet time). However, I think it's a good idea to require that all members go through the encounter-with-God Retreat (second step) and take the how-to-lead-a-cell-group training (fifth step).

### Principle #6: Train everyone as a potential cell leader

When a church concludes that every member is a potential cell leader, the logical step is to train each person to eventually lead a cell group. I quickly acknowledge that not everyone *will* lead a group. There may be a variety of reasons—time pressures and so forth. But as soon as a church accepts the thinking that only certain people *can* lead a group, the church limits itself to subjectively trying to figure out who is the "leader type."[3]

Ideally, each new believer in the church should immediately start attending a cell and begin the equipping track. In reality, it often takes more time. However, the more a church closes the gap between idealism and realism, the more effective it will be.

### Principle #7: Continually adjust and improve the training

The best pastors fine-tune their equipping tracks continually. Cornerstone Church, led by Pastor Gerald Martin, has been perfecting its training track for nine years. My advice is to adapt, adjust, and improve the training system as feedback comes in from those who have taken it.

---

## Sample training track

Pastor Jim Corley at CrossPoint developed his own step-by-step process that is both clear and concise:

### CrossPoint Training Level I

1. Join a cell group.

2. Complete the course *Crossfire* (offered during Sunday school, in a Saturday seminar, or before/after cell).

   **Action step:** Get baptized and become a member.

3. Attend an encounter retreat.

   **Action step:** Break sinful habits.

4. Complete the course *How to Have a Quiet Time* (offered during Sunday school, in a Saturday seminar, or before/after cell).

   **Action step:** Practice regular personal devotions, be assigned an accountability partner by the cell leader, agree to serve as an apprentice cell leader, complete the spiritual life assessment.

5. Complete the course, *How to Evangelize* (offered during Sunday school, in a Saturday seminar, or before/after cell).

   **Action step:** Evangelize and set a launch date for your own cell group.

6. Complete the course *How to Lead a Cell Group* (offered during Sunday school, in a Saturday seminar, or before/after cell).

   **Action step:** Launch cell group.

### CrossPoint Training Level II

1. Be leading an active cell group.
2. Complete the course *How to Study the Bible for Yourself* (offered during Sunday school, in a Saturday seminar, or online).
3. Complete the course *How to Study the Bible for Sharing with Others* (offered during Sunday school, in a Saturday seminar, or online).
4. Complete two of the following courses
   - *The Pentateuch*
   - *The Life of Christ*
   - *The Book of Acts*
   - *The Epistles*

### Action steps for Level II:
- Multiply a cell group at least once.
- Take a short-term missions trip.

### CrossPoint Training Level III

Ministers Study Program (this is a self-study program that is guided by a mentor. It is offered through the Christian and Missionary Alliance, and the goal is for someone to become a licensed Christian worker)

### CrossPoint Training Level IV

Year-long self-funded internship [requirement: having completed stages I–III]

---

## The next generation

I've seen a lot of pastors hesitate in implementing a training track because they're not sure which training track is the best or what material to use. If the pastor is not the creative type, it's best to use someone else's training track material in the beginning. The goal, however, is always to adjust and adapt until the training track is one hundred percent contextualized.

To win the next generation through the cell-driven church, training is essential. When a church concludes that every cell member is a potential cell facilitator, the logical step is to train each person to minister. Training turns members into ministers and gives them confidence to open their homes and penetrate the non-Christian community for Jesus Christ.*

---

* In my book *Leadership Explosion*, I provide in-depth teaching on what is a training track and give many examples of the best training tracks around the world. You can purchase this book at **www.cellchurchsolution.com**, or by calling **1-888-344-CELL**.

## Chapter Eleven

# Coaching

**"B**ut what coaching model should I use?"** asked the bewildered pastor. He had heard of 5x5, G12, and G12.3, and yet he had no idea what was best for him. He didn't know where to start and was ready to throw in the towel. I told him not to worry about the exact coaching structure. "First you have to raise up leaders to coach. When you have leaders to coach, the coaching structures will make sense to you. Right now, the most important thing is to concentrate on the content of coaching."

Most cell churches in North America are not at the point where the coaching structure is very important. What is important is that the coaching actually happens and that the leaders feel coached.

Many pastors feel inadequate in light of the perception that developing a coaching structure is extremely complicated. I try to diffuse their confusion by emphasizing the simplicity of coaching. My goal in this chapter is to highlight the nuts and bolts of coaching, rather than one model of coaching. The *concept* of coaching, rather than the exact coaching *model*, is what North American churches need to understand.

## Coaching as the key

Jim Egli, Ph.D., researched small-group churches around the world and discovered that coaching is the key element for long-term success. Egli did his research among 3000 small-group leaders in twenty countries and discovered that great small-group-based churches prioritized prayer, practiced proactive coaching, and established a culture of multiplication. Yet, when all three components were analyzed together, coaching was the key factor. The difference between groups that start and fizzle and those that make it over the long haul with a vibrant life of multiplication can be summed up in one word: coaching.

Even the best leaders and players need a coach. Michael Jordan needed a coach.[1] Jordan's coach spotted the opposing team's strategy, defended Jordan against over-zealous referees or players, and knew what drills and skills Jordan needed to improve. A coach sees the big picture and can help the player reach his or her full potential.

## Coaching basics

I advise pastors to begin by nailing down the minimum time requirements for the coach to spend with the leader. Once that is established, the coach can progressively learn what to do. I recommend that a lay volunteer coach commit to having a one-on-one meeting with the lay volunteer cell leader once per month and a phone call with the leader once per month. Thus every two weeks the coach would make contact with the cell leader. Establishing the minimum requirements for coaching will help the pastor feel confident that coaching will actually take place.

## Group meetings

Coaching occurs on two levels. The first level is the senior pastor coaching his team. The second level is volunteer lay cell leaders coaching the new leaders who have multiplied new cells.

### The senior pastor and his team

Group coaching meetings are more necessary between senior pastor and his team. If the senior pastor has gathered a paid staff, they should meet weekly. If the senior pastor has gathered a lay volunteer coaching staff, I recommend a group meeting every fifteen days.

During those group coaching meetings, the senior pastor ministers to his key leaders through the Word and prayer. Then the group talks about the cell system by carefully analyzing cell statistics, the training track, multiplication dates, and prayer needs. Like a quarterback in a huddle, the senior pastor directs the cell system through the hub of his leadership team.

### Lay coaches with cell leaders

I encourage lay leaders to continue leading a cell group while coaching up to three cell leaders. I encourage each lay cell coach to call each leader under his or her care once per month and to meet with each person once per month.

In North America that's asking a lot, and thus, group meetings between the lay coach and the lay cell leaders might not be as frequent. I've seen too many "ideal" coaching structures fail because they were based on what should happen rather than what is actually happening. Thus, if time doesn't permit the volunteer coach to have a huddle meeting with cell leaders, by all means the coach should commit to the one-on-one personal time each month and a once a month phone call.

Some churches will have a quarterly huddle with all of the cell leaders present. This is normally directly by the senior pastor.

## Nature of coaching

Effective coaching is all about facilitation rather than teaching. I recommend that coaches perfect the following skills:*

- **Listening.** More than anything else, cell leaders need a coach who is willing to listen to their problems, fears, and needs.
- **Encouragement.** Cell leaders easily face discouragement and need encouragement to keep them going. Great coaches continually encourage cell leaders, acknowledging their important effort and ministry.
- **Care.** Great coaches befriend the cell leaders under their care. They show this care by an occasional birthday card, help on moving day, or any other practical gesture of love and kindness.
- **Development.** Great coaches are constantly resourcing their leaders through email articles, free books, and any type of counsel that will help the cell leader become more effective.
- **Strategizing.** Great coaches plan with the leaders how to multiply the cell group by looking at potential cell leaders in the group, where the new cell will meet, and overcoming obstacles to actually making it happen.
- **Challenging.** Coaches should never allow the leader to be content with mediocrity. "Care-fronting" means speaking the truth in love with improvement as the goal.

---

* My book *How to Be a Great Cell Group Coach* goes into great detail about how to make this happen. See **www.cellchurchsolutions.com**, or call **1-888-344-CELL.**

- **Receiving.** Great coaches receive daily food from Jesus through their personal quiet time. They're filled with the Spirit and then model what they've received from the Master.

## Structure

The largest cell churches in the world follow distinct coaching structures to care for their cell leaders. The main ones are the G12 care structure and the 5x5 structure. The G12 structure promotes one coach for every twelve leaders, following the model of Jesus with His disciples. The 5x5 care structure, otherwise known as the Jethro model, follows Jethro's advice to Moses in Exodus 18 about raising up leaders to care for groups of ten. This approach normally promotes one coach for every five leaders.

My preferred structure is one full-time staff coach for twelve lay cell leaders and one volunteer lay coach for every three cell leaders, while the lay coach continues to lead a normal cell group. I call this care structure the G12.3 care structure.†

## The marathon

Most churches can successfully start groups—even hundreds of them. People will even readily offer their homes—for a few weeks.

To make it over the long haul, however, the small-group leaders must have a high-quality support line, much like the supply line that channels food and other supplies to battle-weary soldiers. The cell-driven strategy succeeds or fails on the quality of the coaching given to the cell leaders.

Small-group ministry is like running a marathon, not a fifty-yard dash. This marathon means maintaining weekly, penetrating cells that continue to grow and multiply. Coaching the cell leaders makes this happen. Without coaching, cell leaders are left to fend for themselves in a spiritual battleground of discouragement, doubt, and frustration. Coaching is the discipline that allows cell ministry to succeed over the long haul.‡

---

† The G12.3 coaching model is explained in my book *From Twelve to Three* and is available for purchase at: **www.cellchurchsolutions.com** or by calling **1-888-344-CELL**.

‡ **www.cellchurchsolutions.com/articles/coaching/coaching.htm** gives additional information about how to coach cell leaders.

## Chapter Twelve

# Priesthood of All Believers

"**J oel, you're placing too much emphasis** on small groups," the board member insisted. "I believe we should focus on developing more ministries in our church—like a social action program—so that people can truly exercise their spiritual gifts."

"But in the small groups they'll have a chance to exercise their gifts," I countered. "Those with the gift of mercy will have the opportunity to reach the poor and needy, and even know personally the people they're trying to reach."

Our conversation that night ended in a stalemate. We both had strong opinions. But the conversation was a blessing in disguise because it forced me to revisit the issue of spiritual gifts and small groups. The conversation stirred me to clarify why I believe small groups are the best place to exercise spiritual gifts.

Many North American churches promote the gifts of the Spirit in the context of ministries within the church. These churches make the assumption that gift usage and church programs/ministries are intimately bound together. That is, if a member is going to use his or her gift, the best place to do so is in church or with a program connected to the church. The progression usually proceeds like this:

1. **A church develops a wide variety of programs and ministries.**
2. **Spiritual gift tests are offered to the members to decide where they can exercise that gift among the ministries and programs that have been created.**
3. **The members are placed within one of the programs and ministries that the church has to offer.**

The problem with this approach is that it's top heavy and ultimately leads to a program-based church. The scriptural context of gift usage is the home.

## New Testament ministry

The main passages of Scripture that talk about the gifts of the Spirit are 1 Corinthians 12, Romans 12, and Ephesians 4. When Paul was writing these epistles, he was writing to house churches—not congregations meeting in a church building. In fact, all the New Testament books were completed by the year AD 90, but the first time the early church had a building of its own was in AD 150. The New Testament was written to house churches in which the exercise of individual gifts was possible.

The home-cell atmosphere enhances the exercise of the gifts of the Spirit. In the intimacy of a small, closely knit group Christians can exercise their spiritual gifts. Eduard Schweizer, a German theologian, said, "The togetherness of the church and its services is not that of a theatre audience, where one or several paid actors act on the stage while everybody else is looking on. Each one takes part with his special gift. . . . It is a body consisting of members . . . asking, challenging, comforting, sharing of Christ and his gifts."[1]

*Effective cell leaders encourage everyone in the cell to use their particular gifts so the body might be edified and non-Christians might be won to Christ.*

Paul the apostle knew that those in the small group (house church) were able to exercise their particular gifts. He could say, "When you come together, everyone has a hymn, or a word of instruction. . ." (I Cor. 14:26).

## Identification of gifts

Scripture says that each believer has a gift (1 Peter 4:10). To discover that gift, a person should begin by reading the key gift passages (1 Cor. 12, Rom. 12, Eph. 4) and books on the subject of spiritual gifts.[2]

Then I encourage a person to exercise his or her spiritual gifts in daily life, especially at the small-group level. One of the main secrets behind discovering spiritual giftedness is trying to determine the "desire level." Exercising a gift should not be a chore. It should be enjoyed. I say to those trying to identify spiritual giftedness: Do you like explaining biblical truth? Perhaps you have the gift of teaching. Do you enjoy praying for people in the group and do you see them healed? Perhaps you have the gift of healing. Do you love to bring refreshments and organize group events? Perhaps you have the gift of helps. Are you drawn to visit cell members who are having problems? Perhaps you have the gift of mercy.

Another key test is confirmation from others. I tell people to look for confirmation from those in the group. What do people confirm in you? Do they notice your capacity to clarify the meaning of Scripture, it's likely that someone will tell you that you have the gift of teaching. My wife's gift of counseling (exhortation) has been confirmed over and over in the small-group environment.

## Use of gifts

I now encourage people to use their gifts primarily in the small group. Effective cell leaders encourage everyone in the cell to use their particular gifts so the body might be edified and non-Christians might be won to Christ.

The person with the gift of teaching might help clarify a difficult passage. The person with the gift of mercy might visit a hurting cell member in the hospital and then mobilize various others to visit that person. The believer with the gift of evangelism might feel compelled to invite friends and relatives or organize a cell outreach.

Cell churches also develop excellent training that helps cell members to discover their spiritual gift(s) with the goal of using those gifts within and outside of the cell group. Debby, for example, has a talent of playing the guitar. Her talent for playing the guitar is empowered by her gift of leadership and prophecy. She faithfully uses her guitar talent playing during the Wednesday night cell meetings.[3]

The celebration wing of the church is often the least effective place to exercise spiritual gifts because only a few believers can actually exercise their gifts in a large-group atmosphere. How many can lead worship? How many can preach? How many can usher? In reality, ministries involved with the celebration wing of the church are limited.

## The priesthood of all believers

The North American postmodern culture emphasizes equal access and participation. While the modern world could be described as the *age of representation*, the postmodern world is the *age of participation*. We live in an age of karaoke. Everyone wants to participate. Everyone can stand up and sing a song. Everyone wants to be involved. Easum, talking about today's emerging church says, "The Priesthood of the believer will finally emerge. Most of the ministry in healthy churches will be done by the laity. Lay pastors will be the norm."[4]

In cell ministry, participation reigns. A pastoral friend of mine has become so excited about cell ministry that he stands up on Sunday and urges his members not to miss the cell meeting during the week. He realizes that everyone can exercise gifts in a cell and that his entire congregation will become priests and ministers of the gospel.

## Chapter Thirteen

# Cells Celebrating on Sunday

**om and Julie were struggling with their marriage,** their children, and relationships in the workplace. Tom was wrestling with sins of pornography and pride, and Julie with depression and the fear of not being an adequate mother. The gathered church on Sunday morning, however, did a poor job of ministering to the needs and hurts of Tom and Julie. They came to church, sat, listened, and left without applying the message to their individual lives.

They needed to go from being spectators to practicing the "one-another" relationships descriptive of Christian fellowship in the Bible. They needed to participate in a life-giving group to fully experience the Christian journey.

I've noticed that many churches in North America don't take advantage of the celebration service to promote cell ministry. There's a tendency to separate the two rather than using the one to promote the other. Because most North American churches prioritize Sunday celebration more than the weekly cell, a great place to start correcting that imbalance is by emphasizing cell life during the celebration.

## Promotion of cell on Sunday

Many, like Tom and Julie, don't know that the cell is the church and is just as important as the Sunday celebration. They get the impression that small-group ministry is just one of the many options to consider—rather than being as important as the celebration service.

The announcements, activities, and church-related tasks all seem to indicate that church priorities reside in activities that take place in the building. Tom and Julie would have a better chance of getting involved in a cell if they knew it was very important.

### Pastor's personal involvement

The lead pastor is the primary channel, although not the only one, to promote cell ministry during the celebration service. He's the gatekeeper through which publicity flows. Granted, in larger churches a variety of people serve under the senior pastor in this area; nevertheless, the senior pastor must guide and direct the flow of information.[1]

---

*Personal involvement (such as leading or attending a cell)*
*allows the pastor to freely add cell examples to sermons.*

---

### Pastor's sermon

Personal involvement (such as leading or attending a cell) allows the pastor to freely add cell examples to sermons. When a pastor who is personally involved in a cell talks about the need for community, body-life evangelism, leadership development, and the use of the gifts of the Spirit, that pastor can tie in personal involvement in cell life, drawing on a variety of illustrations and testimonies from real life.

Soon the congregation begins to realize that cell life is the normal Christian life and that attending the celebration service is only one part of that reality. They soon realize that they must also be involved in cell to capture the full benefits of what the church really is.

### Bulletin

Cell ministry can find a great friend in the bulletin or other advertisements in the church. Some churches don't have a bulletin, but if there's even an occasional handout, it's a great time to give cell ministry its proper place.

I suggest that the bulletin in the cell church highlight a cell testimony of how people's lives have been transformed through cell ministry. Cell announcements should be given priority space so that those visiting will immediately see the heartbeat of the church and know where to go to get involved in a cell group.

I'm coaching one church that has twenty cells and two hundred worshippers. The bulletin, a two-sided sheet of paper, lists all the cell groups each week on the front page. The statement is made each Sunday: We're pastoring our people through cell ministry.

### Announcements and testimonies

Most churches make time for announcements and testimonies. Some churches attach them to the end of the service or before the preaching. Does it make a difference which announcements receive priority? I believe so. In the cell church, cell ministry is central to all that takes place. Why not make it a priority in the announcements? These are some ideas:

- asking a cell member who has been transformed through relational ministry—new friendships, special ministry times—to share what God has done
- hearing the testimony of someone who has received healing within the cell group
- presenting a new multiplication leader to the entire church

Those attending the Sunday celebration need to realize that the primary pastoral services of the church are offered through the cell system. If they need ministry and help, they can find it in a loving cell group.

### Other cell indicators

A visitor to the church should be able to detect the philosophy and priority of the church from the Sunday morning service. Some churches have book tables; larger ones even have bookstores. I encourage cell-based churches to have a cell information table where they lay out relevant books on cell ministry, the weekly cell lesson, a box to place cell reports, and other pertinent information about cell ministry.

It's a great idea to post in the foyer a map of the city with each cell group pinned on it. This map explains where the cells are located, their focus (e.g., family cells, women's cells, youth cells, etc.), and when they meet. A volunteer worker or secretary should be available to answer questions each week and connect new people to cell ministry.[2]

It's not easy to adapt to the cell model. People are accustomed to their old ways and habits. They must be reminded of the cell church focus by what they see in church during the worship service.

## From information to transformation

Tom and Julie's pastor became convinced that cell ministry was the direction for his church to follow. He began leading a cell and practicing the "one anothers" of Scripture that he wanted others to follow. He began to reach out to his neighbors, and soon his sermons included stories of what God was doing in his own life and the life of his cell.

Tom and Julie eventually concluded that if it was important for their pastor to actually lead a cell, they should also give it a try. Since regularly participating in a cell group, Tom and Julie receive weekly personal ministry and a place where they can minister. God has transformed their lives. They marvel at how much their marriage has improved since attending the cell group. They were especially helped by another couple in the cell who openly shared how they learned to communicate better. Tom and Julie noticed how this couple dealt with problems, and they began to do likewise. They now go out on monthly dates and talk through problems and difficulties, rather than argue about them. Church is now lived in relationship with other believers. They've even volunteered to host the cell in their house because they have neighbors they want to invite. They no longer view church as a one hour meeting on Sunday but a lifestyle to be lived 24/7.

## Chapter Fourteen

# Cell Church Planting

**B**ecause books and articles often focus on the mega cell churches around the world, many people equate successful cell church ministry with mega church results.

I admit that my writing has compounded this problem, as my original research focused on the largest cell churches in the world.[1] To discover key principles is one thing; it's quite another thing to say that growing to mega church size is the goal—it's not!

My personal conviction is that exceedingly few cell churches will ever grow to mega cell church status and that church planting should be a far higher priority than expanding one church.

The purpose of this chapter is to stir vision for cell church planting. I believe that the cell church vision in North America will take root only as church planters spread this strategy across the entire continent through new church plants.

## Snapshot of cell church planting

Cell church plants come in different varieties: mother–daughter cell church plants, satellite cell church plants, or just starting a cell from scratch.

The simplicity of cell church planting makes it exciting. Even without a supporting mother church, a church planter can simply open the first cell in a home and begin reaching non-Christians. The cell at this stage is more like a house church. The goal is to see non-Christians come to Christ, be trained through the training track, and then be sent out to lead their own cell groups.

I recommend, however, that the church planter seek to find a team of core members. Each core member should be prepared to eventually start a cell group (or perhaps start one in partnership with another core team member). Where will these core members come from? A few possibilities are the mother church, the denomination, a plea for "missionaries," or help from another church.

The core group meets together in a pilot cell for six months to one year. During that period, the pilot cell of core members practice cell life, using the four Ws as the guide for the cell (welcome, worship, Word, witness). Each core member is encouraged to get to know non-Christians in the neighborhood.

During this same time, the church planter teaches the training track to the core team members apart from the cell itself (see Chapter 10). In our church plant, we found it effective to set apart a Saturday or Sunday for concentrated training.

As the time gets closer to multiplication, the pilot group practices group evangelism (see Chapter 8). When the cell multiplies into several new cells, the church planter concentrates on coaching the new cell leaders (see Chapter 11) while continuing to lead a regular cell group.

I recommend starting monthly celebration services when there are four new cells. Those monthly gatherings might take place in a park, a large house, a school, or church building. When there are eight cells, I recommend a weekly celebration service.

A key part of the DNA from the very beginning is to plant new cell churches.

I've just painted a very brief description of cell church planting. I'm currently writing a new book on cell church planting, which will go into far more detail about the various types of cell church planting and how to do it.[2]

## Return to simplicity

More and more leaders around the world are attracted to a simple form of church life, one that doesn't require huge budgets and super-talented preachers but follows the pattern of the New Testament church. I now find myself desiring a simple, reproducible, New Testament model. And I believe North America needs the same thing.

Tomorrow's cell church won't depend on large buildings or technology to make it work. It will go back to the New Testament rhythm of meeting in celebration and cell.

One reason the mega churches appear so complicated is that they are. One influential mega church in the suburbs of Los Angeles, for example, is embarking on a ten-year expansion project with a 4000-seat worship center, an artificial lake, food court, coffee house, and recreational attractions including a rock-climbing wall and jumbo video screens. The list of activities sounds like the offerings at a Club Med or a small liberal arts college: poetry workshops, creative writing, singles groups, job fairs, vocational training, musical lessons, and even auto repair clinics.[3]

---

*The beauty of a simple cell church is that it's reproducible.*

---

The beauty of a simple cell church is that it's reproducible.

A person who has led a cell, multiplied it, and coached the daughter-cell leader(s) has completed the core basics of cell church planting. Such a person is a prime candidate for future church planting—anywhere in the world.

Undoubtedly, this same person will seek out biblical education and grow in the knowledge of Jesus Christ. Fruitfulness on the cell level builds confidence for future church planting and allows the candidate to then make it happen. The order is clear cut:

- **Attend a cell.**
- **Receive training.**
- **Plant a cell.**
- **Multiply the cell several times.**
- **Coach the leaders who have multiplied out.**
- **Receive higher-level biblical training.**
- **Plant a church in the U.S. or overseas using the same strategy.**

Cell churches don't require a huge budget, a large plot of land, modern buildings, or super-talented pastors. The cell strategy uses the houses of people all over the city as the primary meeting locations. Instead of laboring to get people out of their houses once a week for an hour-long service, it seeks to utilize those same houses to penetrate an entire city and nation.

In May 2002 I spoke to denominational executives who were highly influenced by the house church movement. They resisted the idea of the mega church because of the mega problems associated with this phenomenon: mega buildings, mega land space, and bureaucratic nightmare of mega proportions.

I encouraged these leaders not to reject large cell churches altogether. "After all," I told them, "if God calls a pastor who can lead a cell church to mega church status as a flagship church, such a church could have a powerful influence." Bethany World Prayer Center is one of those examples. Mega cell churches, however, shouldn't be the norm or the goal. In my list of successful cell churches (see Chapter 5), only two of the forty-four churches grew to mega status. The vast majority of cell church pastors will have smaller, more nimble churches that focus on church planting.

## Getting the job done

Christian Schwarz and Natural Church Development research have made it crystal clear that church plants do a much better job of actually winning souls, baptizing members, and ministering to particular needs than the mega churches—they are 1600 times more effective![4]

Larry Kreider, founder of DOVE, is a model of developing cell church planting leaders. Kreider has spawned more than one hundred churches around the world. His book, *Helping You Build Cell Churches: A Comprehensive Training Manual for Pastors, Cell Leaders and Church Planters*, talks about how to plant churches.[5] Kreider refused to hold on to one mega cell church; rather, he decentralized the churches all over the globe.

Jamey Miller, pastor of Christ Fellowship, has planted nine cell churches since 1993. The mother church has 300 in celebration attendance. Miller's commitment to developing leaders through cells flows naturally into church planting. Other cell churches listed in Chapter 5 did the same thing. I believe this will be the model for future church growth.

John Church, the most effective North American youth cell pastor I know, recently left the youth cell ministry at Cypress Creek Church (CCC) to obtain further theological training and *plant his own church*.

While John was still on staff at CCC, I talked with him about the gap he would leave when he departed. He fired back, "We have raised up the youth pastor to take my place from among those who have gone through our youth training. He has been very fruitful, and I believe he'll even do a better job than I."

The church didn't miss a beat, mainly because John Church had already raised up a Timothy to replace him. Those, like John Church, who have successfully multiplied cell groups, are prime candidates to plant cell churches. Churches like Cypress Creek Church are positioned to send out leaders to make it happen.

Many, many leaders of various degrees of talent, education, and gifting can grow a reproducing cell church—if they have been successful at the cell level. Effective cell church pastors excel in making disciples who make disciples.

If we see church planting in terms of multiplying cells and bringing those cells together for worship, we've reached the potential of the priesthood of all believers and we're on the precipice of an explosion of growth and blessing. The church of the future dares to believe that each member is a potential cell leader and to envision a cell-church-planting movement that makes disciples who make disciples.

## Putting it all together

In this last section we've looked at unique cell church principles that need to be emphasized in North America—beginning with prayer and ending with church planting.

Throughout this book, I've made the point that cell church is no quick-fix solution. Rather it's a radical call to discipleship, evangelism, and multiplication. Yet the cell-driven church is also the healthiest strategy, and thus it's worth every bit of effort to make it happen.

This book doesn't stop here. It continues to the next step in the journey. As you connect to **www.cellchurchsolutions.com**, we hope to help you become all God wants you to be. CCS is committed to the process of helping churches adapt to cell ministry and plant cell churches throughout North America and beyond. It will do this by providing resources, coaching, and other ministry opportunities.

The cell-driven strategy is what North America needs to send forth laborers to plant new churches. As cell churches lead the way, I see a brighter day for the church in North America. I envision the day that North America will once again grow vital, healthy churches that are sending bases for world evangelism.

# Resource List

**Joel Comiskey's previous books cover the following topics**

- Leading a cell group (*How to Lead a Great Cell Group Meeting, 2001*).
- How to multiply the cell group (*Home Cell Group Explosion, 1998*).
- How to prepare spiritually for cell ministry (*An Appointment with the King, 2002*).
- How to practically organize your cell system (*Reap the Harvest, 1999; Cell Church Explosion, 2004*).
- How to train future cell leaders (*Leadership Explosion, 2001*).
- How to coach/care for cell leaders (*How to be a Great Cell Group Coach, 2003; Groups of Twelve, 2000; From Twelve to Three, 2002*).
- How to fine tune your cell system (*Making Cell Groups Work Navigation Guide, 2003*).
- Principles from the second largest church in the world (*Passion and Persistence, 2004*).

All of the books listed are available from Cell Church Solutions by calling toll-free **1-888-344-CELL** (2355) or by ordering online at: **www.CellChurchSolutions.com**.

## More Cell Church Solutions Resources by Joel Comiskey

**Making Cell Groups Work Navigation Guide:** *A Toolbox of Ideas and Strategies for Transforming Your Church*

For the first time, experts in cell group ministry have come together to provide you with a 600 page reference tool like no other. When Ralph Neighbour, Bill Beckham, Joel Comiskey and Randall Neighbour compiled new articles and information under careful orchestration and in-depth understanding that Scott Boren brings to the table, it's as powerful as private consulting! Joel Comiskey has an entire book within this mammoth 600 page work. There are also four additional authors.

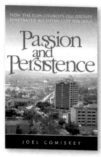

**Passion and Persistence:** *How the Elim Church's Cell Groups Penetrated an Entire City for Jesus*

This book describes how the Elim Church in San Salvador grew from a small group to 116,000 people in 10,000 cell groups. Comiskey takes the principles from Elim and applies them to churches in North America and all over the world. Ralph Neighbour says: "I believe this book will be remember as one of the most important ever written about a cell church movement! I experienced the "passion" when visiting Elim many years ago. As described by Joel Comiskey, Elim's passion is more than an atmosphere: it is perfume! Their cells exude a "sweet smell, a sacrifice pleasing to God" (Philippians 4:18). Their Basic Christian Communities are filled with the presence and power of Christ. That is why they have multiplied not only in one culture but in many, spreading the aroma around the world. Best of all, this report about Elim is not a "pattern" to be slavishly copied. It is a journey into grasping the true theology and methodology of the New Testament church." You'll discover how the Elim Church fans into flame their passion for Jesus and His Word, how they organize their cells to penetrate a city and world for Jesus, and how they persist until God brings the fruit. 158 pgs.

**How to be a Great Cell Group Coach:** *Practical insight for Supporting and Mentoring Cell Group Leaders*

Research has proven that the greatest contributor to cell group success is the quality of coaching provided for cell group leaders. Many are serving in the position of a coach, but they don't fully understand what they are supposed to do in this position. Joel Comiskey has identified seven habits of great cell group coaches. These include: Receiving from God, Listening to the needs of the cell group leader, Encouraging the cell group leader, Caring for the multiple aspects of a leader's life, Developing the cell leader in various aspects of leadership, Strategizing with the cell leader to create a plan, Challenging the cell leader to grow.

Practical insights on how to develop these seven habits are outlined in section one. Section two addresses how to polish your skills as a coach with instructions on diagnosing problems in a cell group, how to lead coaching meetings, and what to do when visiting a cell group meeting. This book will prepare you to be a great cell group coach, one who mentors, supports, and guides cell group leaders into great ministry. 139 pgs.

### From Twelve To Three: How to Apply G12 Principles in Your Church

The concept of the Groups of 12 began in Bogota, Colombia, but now it is sweeping the globe. Joel Comiskey has spent years researching the G12 structure and the principles behind it. From his experience as a pastor, trainer, and consultant, he has discovered that there are two ways to embrace the G12 concept: adopting the entire model or applying the principles that support the model. This book focuses on the application of principles rather than adoption of the entire model. It outlines the principles and provides a modified application which Joel calls the G12.3. This approach presents a pattern that is adaptable to many different church contexts. The concluding section illustrates how to implement the G12.3 in various kinds of churches, including church plants, small churches, large churches, and churches that already have cells. 178 pgs.

### How To Lead A Great Cell Group Meeting: So People Want to Come Back

Do people expectantly return to your group meetings every week? Do you have fun and experience joy during your meetings? Is everyone participating in discussion and ministry? You can lead a great cell group meeting, one that is life changing and dynamic. Most people don't realize that they can create a God-filled atmosphere because they don't know how. Now the secret is out. This guide will show you how to:

- Prepare yourself spiritually to hear God during the meeting
- Structure the meeting so it flows
- Spur people in the group to participate and share their lives openly
- Share your life with others in the group
- Create stimulating questions
- Listen effectively to discover what is transpiring in others' lives
- Encourage and edify group members
- Open the group to non-Christians
- See the details that create a warm atmosphere

By implementing these time-tested ideas, your group meetings will become the hot-item of your members' week. They will go home wanting more and return each week bringing new people with them. 140 pgs.

**Groups of Twelve:** *A New Way to Mobilize Leaders and Multiply Groups in Your Church*

This book clears the confusion about the Groups of 12 model. Joel dug deeply into the International Charismatic Mission in Bogota, Colombia and other G12 churches to learn the simple principles that G12 has to offer your church. This book also contrasts the G12 model with the classic 5x5 and shows you what to do with this new model of ministry. Through onsite research, international case studies and practical experience, Joel Comiskey outlines the G12 principles that your church can use today. 182 pgs.

**An Appointment with the King:** *Ideas for Jump-Starting Your Devotional Life*

With full calendars and long lists of things to do, people often put on hold life's most important goal: building an intimate relationship with God. Often, believers wish to pursue the goal but are not sure how to do it. They feel frustrated or guilty when their attempts at personal devotions seem empty and unfruitful. With warm, encouraging writing, Joel Comiskey guides readers on how to set a daily appointment with the King and make it an exciting time they will look forward to. This book first answers the question 'Where do I start?' with step-by-step instructions on how to spend time with God and practical ideas for experiencing him more fully. Second, it highlights the benefits of spending time with God, including joy, victory over sin, and spiritual guidance. Third, this book inspires and motivates those who already have a quiet time to press ahead and grow in their intimacy with God. An Appointment with the King discusses personal priorities, the use of Scripture, listening, place and time of day, meditation, increased power in prayer, and other helpful topics related to daily quiet time. The book will help Christians tap into God's resources on a daily basis, so that even in the midst of busyness they can walk with him in intimacy and abundance. 175 pgs.

**Home Cell Group Explosion:** *How Your Small Group Can Grow and Multiply*

Home Cell Group Explosion is the most researched and practical book every written on cell group ministry! Joel Comiskey traversed the globe to find out why certain churches and small groups are successful in reaching the lost. He found the answers and freely shares them within this volume. If you are a pastor or small group leader, you should devour this book! It will encourage you and give you simple, practical steps for dynamic small group life and growth. 175 pgs.

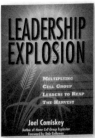

**Leadership Explosion:** *Multiplying Cell Group Leaders to Reap the Harvest*

Some have said that cell groups are leader breeders. Yet even the best cell groups often have a leadership shortage. This shortage impedes growth and much of the harvest goes untouched. Joel Comiskey has discovered why some churches are better at raising up new cell leaders than others. These churches do more than pray and hope for new leaders. They have an intentional strategy, a plan that will quickly equip as many new leaders as possible. In this book, you will discover the training models these churches use to multiply leaders. You will discover the underlying principles of these models so that you can apply them. 202 pgs.

"Joel has the divine ability to take vital kingdom information compiled from throughout the body of Christ and boil it down so churches can clearly understand and practically apply these truths. I highly recommend this book for everyone who is serious about training leaders for the harvest."
— LARRY KREIDER, International Director, DOVE Christian Fellowship International

**Reap The Harvest:** *How a Small Group System Can Grow Your Church*

Have you tried small groups and hit a brick wall? Have you wondered why your groups are not producing the fruit that was promised? Are you looking to make your small groups more effective? Cell-church specialist and pastor Dr. Joel Comiskey studied the world's most successful cell churches to determine why they grow. They key: They have embraced specific principles. Conversely, churches that do not embrace these same principles have problems with their groups and therefore do not grow. Cell churches are successful not because they have small groups but because they have the system in place to support the groups. In Reap the Harvest, you will discover how these systems work. 236 pgs.

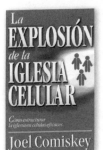

**La Explosión de la Iglesia Celular:** *Cómo Estructurar la Iglesia en Células Eficaces* (Editorial Clie, 2004)

This book is only available in Spanish and contains Joel Comiskey's research of eight of the world's largest cell churches—five of which reside in Latin America. It details how to make the transition from a traditional church to the cell church structure and many other valuable insights, including: the history of the cell church, how to organize your church to become a praying church, the most important principles of the cell church, and how to raise up an army of cell leaders.

# Index

# Endnotes

## Introduction

1 The official definition of North America includes Greenland, Canada, the United States, and Mexico. However, the total population of Greenland (2003 estimate) is 56 385, and thus I didn't feel the need to include this island in the focus group. For those living in Mexico, my books *Groups of Twelve* (case study of the International Charismatic Mission in Bogota, Colombia) and *Passion and Persistence* (case study of the Elim Church in San Salvador) apply more specifically to their situation.

2 G12 means group of twelve and is a coaching structure to care for cell leaders patterned after Christ's care for His disciples. My books *Groups of Twelve* (Houston, TX: Touch Publications, 1999) and *From Twelve to Three* (Houston, TX: Touch Publications, 2002) go into much more detail about the G12 movement.

3 There are a few books based on research of the cell church in North American, including books by Dale Galloway and a new book by Scott Boren titled *Making Cell Groups Work* (Houston, TX: Touch Publications, 2002).

4 Received in my inbox through cellchurchtalk, an Internet email group dedicated to cell church issues. Gary Penny wrote this in May 1998.

5 The 5x5 care structure approach normally calls for one coach for every five leaders.

6 For an update on our progress, please visit www.comiskey.org and www.wellspringcellchurch.org.

7 Will McRaney, "The Evangelistic Conversation in an Increasingly Postmodern America," *Journal of the American Society for Church Growth* (Winter 2001), p. 86.

## Chapter 1

1 A friend of mine who is superintendent over some 70 Methodist churches in southern California took a week-long doctoral course with George Barna at APU. He said, "George [Barna] is very discouraged— perhaps even depressed over the state of the North American church. It is an easy state to enter. Perhaps this is what Jeremiah felt."

2 Leonard Sweet, *SoulTsunami* (Grand Rapids, MI: Zondervan Publishing House, 1999), p. 50.

3 George Barna, "Number of unchurched adults has nearly doubled since 1991," Accessed on Wednesday, May 5, 2004 at http://www.barna.org/FlexPage.aspx?Page=BarnaUpdateNarrow&BarnaUpdateID=163. Barna's definition of unchurched: "not having attended a Christian church service, other than for a holiday service, such as Christmas or Easter, or for special events such as a wedding or funeral, at any time in the past six months." The proportion of those in this category has risen from 21% in 1991 to 34% today.

4 Tom Clegg and Warren Bird, *Lost in America: Helping Your Friends Find Their Way Home*, as quoted in *Journal for the American Society for Church Growth*, Spring 2001, p. 68.

5 Tom Clegg and Warren Bird, *Lost in America: How Your Church Can Impact the World Next Door*, Loveland, CO: Group Publishing, Inc, 2000), p.33.

6 Clegg and Bird, *Lost in America: How Your Church Can Impact the World Next Door*, pp. 25–27.

7 Tom Sine, *Mustard Seed Faith versus McWorld* (Grand Rapids, MI: Baker Books, 1999), p. 135. The statistics here represent the U.S. church. Canadian church attendance is much lower.

8 "Poll: Protestant majority in U.S. eroding dropped from 63 percent to 52 percent in a decade," © 2004 The Associated Press. Accessed on Tuesday, July 20, 2004 at http://www.msnbc.msn.com/id/5465761/.

9 The June 2004 edition of *Outreach* magazine highlighted the proliferation of mega churches in the U.S. The article says that the phenomenon of churches with attendance of more than 3000 is exploding in the U.S.

10 *USA Today*, October 23, 1997 as quoted in McRaney, *Journal of the American Society for Church Growth*, p. 81.

11 Eddie Gibbs, *Church Next* (Downer's Grove, IL: InterVarsity Press, 2000), p. 41.

12 Clegg and Bird, as quoted in *Journal for the American Society for Church Growth*, pp. 58–59.

13 Clegg and Bird, as quoted in *Journal for the American Society for Church Growth*, p. 60.

14 As quoted in Randy Frazee, *The Connecting Church* (Zondervan Publishing House: Grand Rapids, MI, 2001), p. 13.

15 Gibbs, *Church Next*, p. 154.

16 Clegg and Bird, as quoted in *Journal for the American Society for Church Growth*, p. 61.

17 George Barna report, Accessed on Wednesday, January 14, 2004 at http://www.barna.org/cgi-bin/PagePressRelease.asp?PressReleaseID=156&Reference=A. Of the nation's 320 000 Protestant churches, more than 42 000 are Southern Baptist and more than 35 000 are United Methodist; these two denominations alone account for roughly one-quarter of all Protestant churches in the U.S. The Southern Baptists had the highest percentage of pastors with a biblical worldview (71%) while the Methodists were lowest among the seven segments evaluated (27%). Among the other segments examined, 57% of the pastors of Baptist churches (other than Southern Baptist) had a biblical worldview, as did 51% of non-denominational Protestant pastors, 44% of pastors of charismatic or Pentecostal churches, 35% of pastors of black churches, and 28% of pastors leading mainline congregations. The most intriguing finding relates to theological training. Educationally, the pastors least likely to have a biblical worldview are those who are seminary graduates (45%). In contrast, three out of five pastors who have not attended seminary operate with a biblical worldview (59%).

18 "The most important point," Barna argued, "is that you can't give people what you don't have. The low percentage of Christians who have a biblical worldview is a direct reflection of the fact that half of our primary religious teachers and leaders do not have one."

19 Clegg and Bird, as quoted in *Journal for the American Society for Church Growth*, p. 67. New findings by Barna, "Born Again Christians Just As Likely to Divorce As Are Non-Christians," September 8, 2004. Accessed on Wednesday, September 08, 2004 at http://www.barna.org/FlexPage.aspx?Page=BarnaUpdateNarrow&BarnaUpdateID=170. "A new study released by The Barna Group, of Ventura, California, shows that the likelihood of married adults getting divorced is identical among born again Christians and those who are not born again. The study also cited attitudinal data showing that most Americans reject the notion that divorce is a sin."

20 George Barna, "Number of unchurched adults has nearly doubled since 1991," Accessed on Wednesday, May 05, 2004 at http://www.barna.org/FlexPage.aspx?Page=BarnaUpdateNarrow&BarnaUpdateID=163.

21 George Barna updates, accessed on March 01, 2004 at http://www.barna.org/cgi-bin/PagePressRelease.asp?PressReleaseID=159&Reference=A

22 Dale Hurd, "A Tidal Wave of Christianity," *CBN News Sr. Reporter*. Accessed on Monday, August 02, 2004 at http://www.cbn.com/CBNNews/News/030819a.asp.

## Chapter 2

1 Bill Easum, "Emerging Trends for Effective Ministry in the 21st Century, *Journal for the American Society for Church Growth*, Spring 2001, p. 41.

2 Lawrence Khong, *The Apostolic Cell Church: Practical Strategies for Growth and Outreach from the Story of Faith Community Baptist Church* (Singapore: Touch Ministries International, 2000), p. 38.

3 George Barna as quoted in Julie Gorman, *Community that is Christian* (Wheaton, IL: Victor Books, 1993), p. 81.

4 Robert Wuthnow, *I Come Away Stronger: How Small Groups Are Shaping American Religion* (Grand Rapids, MI: Eerdmans Publishing Company, 1994), p. 45. Robert Wuthnow's ground-breaking survey of small groups in the U.S. not only discovered that 40% of the U.S. adult population is involved in a small group, but that 7% who were not currently in a small group planned on joining one within the following year.

5 Lyle E. Schaller, *The New Reformation: Tomorrow Arrived Yesterday* (Nashville, TN: Abingdon Press, 1995), p. 14.

6 Sherwood G. Lingenfelter and Marvin K. Mayers, *Ministering Cross-Culturally* (Grand Rapids, MI: Baker Book House, 1986), p. 83.

7 James Lardner, "World-class Workaholics," *U.S. News & World Report* (December 20, 1999).

8 Mahatma Gandhi once said, "I like your Christ, but I do not like your Christians. Your Christians are so unlike your Christ." Generation Next first wants to see the real Jesus lived out in authentic Christians; they will then go and do likewise.

9 Hugh Clay Paulk, "Serendipitous Stats," sent to my personal email by Cliff Bowman on Tuesday, July 22, 2003.

10 "Earth in 2050: Expect 9 billion humans," Associated Press. Accessed at http://www.msnbc.msn.com/id/5732657/ on Tuesday, August 17, 2004. This is a growth rate of 43%.

11 Phuong Ly, "Faith Minority Pastors Preach Diversity, Clergy of Color Help Expand Horizons of White Churches." Accessed from the Washington Post web site at http://www.washingtonpost.com/wp-dyn/articles/A47380-2004Apr3_2.html on Sunday, April 04, 2004.

12 George Barna, "Ethnic Groups Differ Substantially On Matters of Faith," Accessed on Tuesday, August 10, 2004. Posted on Barna's web site: http://www.barna.org/FlexPage.aspx?Page=BarnaUpdate&BarnaUpdateID=169. The white population of the U.S. is the largest racial group (68%) but also the slowest growing. The fastest growing are the Hispanic (currently 14% of the U.S. population) and Asian populations (4%), with the black population experiencing moderate growth (13%). The overwhelming size of the white population often obscures the significant gaps in belief and practice among the different racial groups.

13 Khong, *The Apostolic Cell Church*, p., 109.

## Chapter 3

1 Christian Schwarz, *Natural Church Development* (Carol Steam, IL: ChurchSmart Resources, 1996). The research was conducted in thirty-two countries in North and South America, Africa, Asia, Australia, and Europe (western and eastern).

2 Page 16 of Les Brickman's *Natural Church Development and Cell Church: Friend or Foe?* (Seoul, Korea: NCD Publishers, 2004) lists a more complete analysis of the principles:

### 1. Empowering Leadership
Effective leadership begins with an intimate relationship with God, resulting in Christ-like character and a clear sense of God's calling for leaders' lives. As this base of spiritual maturity increases,

effective pastors and leaders multiply, guide, empower, and equip disciples to realize their full potential in Christ and work together to accomplish God's vision.

2. **Gift-Oriented Ministry**

The Holy Spirit sovereignly gives to every Christian spiritual gift(s) for the building of God's kingdom. Church leaders have the responsibility to help believers discover, develop, and exercise their gifts in appropriate ministries so that the Body of Christ "grows and builds itself up in love."

3. **Passionate Spirituality**

Effective ministry flows out of a passionate spirituality. Spiritual intimacy leads to a strong conviction that God will act in powerful ways. A godly vision can only be accomplished through an optimistic faith that views obstacles as opportunities and turns defeats into victories.

4. **Functional Structures**

The Church is the living Body of Christ. Like all healthy organisms, it requires numerous systems that work together to fulfill its intended purpose. Each must be evaluated regularly to determine if it is still the best way to accomplish the intended purpose.

5. **Inspiring Worship**

Inspiring Worship is a personal and corporate encounter with the living God. Both personal and corporate worship must be infused with the presence of God resulting in times of joyous exultation and times of quiet reverence. Inspiring worship is not driven by a particular style or ministry focus group—but rather the shared experience of God's awesome presence.

6. **Holistic Small Groups**

Holistic small groups are disciple-making communities which endeavor to reach the unchurched, meet individual needs, develop each person according to their God-given gifts and raise leaders to sustain the growth of the church. Like healthy body cells, holistic small groups are designed to grow and multiply.

7. **Need-Oriented Evangelism**

Need-oriented evangelism intentionally cultivates relationships with pre-Christian people so they can become fully-devoted followers of Jesus Christ who are actively participating within the life of the church and community. Using appropriate ministries and authentic relationships, believers can guide others into the family of God.

8. **Loving Relationships**

Loving relationships are the heart of a healthy, growing church. Jesus said people will know we are His disciples by our love. Practical demonstration of love builds authentic Christian community and brings others into God's kingdom.

3  Christoph Schalk wrote to me on Tuesday, August 31, 2004, saying there were 30 157 711 data entries in the NCD database.

4  "Cell Churches and the NCD survey," *CoachNet: The Cell Church Chronicles*, October 2002. Concerning this study, Christoph Schalk, the primary statistician of NCD and author of this recent comparative study, said, "We had to use a criteria that comes close to the definition of a cell church. There is a question in our survey that asks what percentage of the worship service attendees are members of a small group. So, here is our pragmatic definition: Cell churches = churches with more than 75% of the worship service attendance being members of small groups."

5  Email from Christoph Schalk on Monday, April 19, 2004. He said, "Here's the answer to your question: 100% of these churches with more than 75% in small groups do have holistic small groups, and have an average score in holistic small groups higher than 65."

6  Schwarz, *Natural Church Development*, p. 32.

7 Brickman, *Natural Church Development and Cell Church: Friend or Foe?* On page 8 he says, "I am suggesting a marriage between the principles of cell church and Natural Church Development. I am suggesting not only compatibility, but I am suggesting that if a cell church paradigm can chase a thousand, the union of a cell church paradigm with the NCD paradigm can chase ten thousand. The whole will be far greater than the sum of the parts."

8 Ultimately, the goal is that those in the training track graduate and lead their own cells. The process continues, allowing a steady stream of servant leaders to serve in the church.

## Chapter 4

1 Roberta Hestenes, a small-group pioneer, opened her presentation at a small-group conference in southern California by thanking all the speakers for their contribution to the small-group movement and then humbly acknowledging that everyone copies from each other. When I heard her say this, I was reminded of the quote by Philip Johnson, a famous author who said, "You always copy. Everybody copies, whether they admit it or not. There is no such thing as not copying. There are so few original ideas in the world that you don't have to worry about them. Creativity is selective copying" (as quoted in Kenneth Atchity, *A Writer's Time*, New York: W.W. Norton Company, 1995, p. 226). I owe much in my own small-group journey to people like David Cho, Carl George, Ralph Neighbour, and Larry Stockstill. In large part, my own thinking comes from wrestling with their thoughts and ideas.

2 Cho emphasized a geographically based care structure, and it's interesting that today some are reviving the geographical model. I'm referring to Randy Frazee's geographically based model found in his book *The Connecting Church*.

3 Carl George, *The Coming Church Revolution* (Grand Rapids, MI: Fleming H. Revell, 1994), pp. 69–70.

4 David Limiero, "Meta, Model, or Martyr? Three Approaches to Introducing a Small Groups Ministry in Your Church," July 1996. http://smallgroups.com/models07.htm. Accessed: Friday, May 22, 1998.

5 The Free Market model developed by Ted Haggard has largely followed Meta thinking by offering an enormous platter of small groups that start and stop on a semester basis.

6 Bethany's senior pastor, Larry Stockstill, is now a member of César Castellanos's international group of twelve. Jubilee Christian Center (senior pastor Dick Bernal) in San Jose, California has fully adopted the G12 model.

7 I believe this is far too limiting. God wants each leader to experience the same creativity as Castellanos and even go beyond what he is doing. Following a particular model, rather than principles, can cause a church to fall several steps behind. Once a church or leader gets under "the model," an entrapment can occur because creativity becomes dulled and the pastor begins to look to others—rather than the Holy Spirit—for the next step.

8 The ICM training materials have many positive characteristics. Yet every church should take the liberty to adapt its material, just like ICM adapted Cho's material to make it better. I'm saddened that ICM won't freely sell their material unless a church commits itself to follow it one hundred percent.

9 Though the cell church has always had gender-specific small groups, it seems that ICM and those following their exact model are now under-emphasizing family cells (which are a crying need in today's society).

10 The term "Radical Middle" was used to describe the history of the Vineyard movement in Bill Jackson's book *The Quest for the Radical Middle* (Cape Town, South Africa: Vineyard International Publishing, 1999). One day on the phone I was talking with Scott Boren, my editor for many years at Touch Publications, about balance in cell ministry. Scott used the phrase "Radical Middle," and it stuck in my mind as the best descriptive phrase to describe a new way of thinking in the cell church today.

11 Three cell champions who stand out are Floyd Schwanz, Jim Egli, and Jerry Popenhagen. Boren, in *Making Cell Groups Work*, pp. 113–115, talks about the role of the cell champion. Boren defines this person as, "A person with a special passion for cell group ministry, who has a submissive heart and can work in unity with the senior pastor." The senior pastor must always maintain the cell church vision and personally be involved with cell ministry in order to practice what he preaches. Yet a cell champion will stay on the cutting edge of cell ministry, providing resources and personal passion to keep the cell flame burning brightly.

12 Some churches (e.g., Church of Christ or Christian Church) don't have one senior pastor; they have a team of pastors/leaders and one preaching pastor. I've seen cell church work in this environment as long as the top elders or leaders are fully behind the vision.

13 Dale Galloway, *The Small Group Book* (Grand Rapids, MI: Fleming H. Revell, 1995), p. 21.

14 I like to make comparisons between the cell and Sunday worship. The reason a pastor wants his people to regularly come to Sunday worship—and not just haphazardly meet with someone at Pizza Hut to pray together—is because the pastor knows the people will hear a biblically based message and worship in a quality controlled environment.

15 Kenneth Scott Latourette, *A History of Christianity*, Vol. 2, (New York: Harper & Row Publishers, 1975), p. 1026.

16 George Hunter III, *To Spread the Power: Church Growth in the Wesleyan Spirit*, (Nashville, TN: Abingdon Press 1987), p. 84.

## Chapter 5

1 Each church must update itself on Touch's cell church web service every six months or the name of the church is removed from the list. Only current cell churches, therefore, are listed.

2 Michael Green, ed., *Church without Walls: A global examination of cell church* Carlisle, Cumbria, UK: Paternoster Press, 2002), pp. 133.

3 NCD testing is not free of charge and requires that a church or denomination take various steps to ensure quality control.

4 The data from Christian Schwarz's research team in Germany suggests that cell churches averaged 2.5 churches planted compared to 1.9 churches planted for non-cell churches.

5 As a result of this ministry, Seibert, along with others from the college ministries, wrote the book, *Reaching College Students through Cells: A practical training tool for college cell leaders from Highland Baptist College Ministries* (Houston, TX: Touch Publications, 1997).

6 Carl Everett, who heads up Bethany Cell Church Network, wrote on Tuesday, August 24, 2004, "Last year through the G12 Global plants, we planted 1009 churches. This year we have planted 326 churches. We are planting on the average of 1 church every 12 hours." For more information on the global G12 project, please see www.global12project.com.

7 Larry Stockstill, *The Cell Church* (Ventura, CA: Regal Books, 1998), pp. 136. The book outlines what a church can do to build a vibrant, relevant, and workable cell church. The book identifies the key principles that have catapulted Bethany World Prayer Center from a respectable church of twenty-five ingrown "fellowship" groups to a dynamic church of 800 multiplying cell groups. In the first chapter Stockstill relates his own pilgrimage:

- 1992 read Neighbour's book *Where Do We Go From Here* (derived principles)
- 1993 visited Faith Community Baptist in Singapore (copied the cell office structure)
- 1993 visited Yoido Full Gospel Church in Seoul, Korea (understood care/growth structure)
- 1993 visited Elim Church in El Salvador (understood the importance of evangelism in cells)

For years Stockstill juggled numerous church programs. He says on pp. 29–30: "As the pastor of a church with cells, I was like the juggler who performed on the Ed Sullivan show years ago. He could spin a plate and put it on a stick, repeating that process 15 to 20 times. The catch was, however, that the juggler had to constantly run back and forth to spin each plate or it would fall. His personal momentum was necessary to keep all the plates aloft."

Chapter eight delineates seven key principles of the G12 model that Bethany was following at the time. (Since the book was published they have moved to a pure G12 model.) Stockstill speaks from his heart in the chapter called "Dangers and Challenges." He covers financial impropriety in cell meetings, unapproved teaching, backsliding and burnout, children in cells, and other important themes.

8 Jay Firebaugh has an excellent tape series called *The Key is the Coach: Practical Steps to Successful Coaching* (Houston, TX: Touch Outreach Ministries, 1999). A manual comes with the four-cassette series.

9 This church's worldwide statistics are 220 cells, 2750 worship attendance in 30 network churches and church plants, 3500 total membership.

10 Boren, *Making Cell Groups Work*, pp. 113–115. He talks about the role of the cell champion. Boren defines this person as, "A person with a special passion for cell group ministry, who has a submissive heart and can work in unity with the senior pastor." The senior pastor must always maintain the cell church vision and personally be involved with cell ministry to practice what he preaches. Yet a cell champion—like Floyd Schwanz—will stay on the cutting edge of cell ministry, providing resources and personal passion to keep the cell flame burning brightly.

11 Floyd Schwanz, *Growing Small Groups* (Kansas City, Missouri: Beacon Hill Press, 1995), pp. 213.

12 The simplicity and power of their approach can be found on their web site, which declares, "We are structured as a church of cells and celebration. Our cells (small groups) meet weekly in homes and are places where people, in any stage of life, can come together to discover more about who God is and how He can make a difference in their lives. The congregation meets for corporate worship on Sunday mornings at 9 and 11 a.m."

## Chapter 7

1 Jonathan Stuart Campbell, *A Postmodern Challenge: The Gospel and Church in Changing Culture*. A tutorial course in mission theology. Fuller Theological Seminary, March, 1996, p. 54.

2 Robert D. Putman, *Bowling Alone* (New York: Simon & Schuster, 2000), p. 284.

3 And there is nothing quite like the atmosphere of a home to confirm the fact that we are, indeed, God's family. The atmosphere of the home has a way of confirming our familial relationship. The home adds a distinct flavor of family living (decorations, furniture, kitchen, etc.). It doesn't take long to taste and feel the presence of family interaction. As a result, cell members warm up to each other much more quickly in the atmosphere of a home than they would during a similar meeting in the church.

4 Larry Crabb, *Connecting* (Nashville, TN: Word Publishing, 1997), p. 31.

## Chapter 8

1 Eddie Gibbs, "Churches in Cultural Transition," *Strategies for Today's Leaders* (Summer, 2000), p. 7.

2 McRaney, *Journal of the American Society for Church Growth*, p. 91.

3 Rob sent the following email to me on July 25, 2002: "Our cells evangelize by building relationships with people outside the family of God—family, friends, co-workers, neighbors, school mates, etc. We build authentic relationships, love people, pray hard, and do 'teamwork' evangelism. I was struck one day by the pattern of evangelism in the NT—Jesus sends out the 12, 2x2. He sends out the 70, 2x2. You get to the book of Acts and it's Peter and John, Paul and Barnabas, Paul and Timothy, Paul and Luke, Paul

and Silas (Paul and everybody), but it's always in teams. The only exception that I can think of is Philip ('The Evangelist'). Yet, we Americans do evangelism like we do everything else, in isolation, clinging to our individualism. So, we train, teach, and practice 'teamwork' evangelism. I build a relationship with my friend Jon. Jon likes golf, so I invite other members of my cell to play golf with my friend Jon. You've seen the church growth stuff about if someone doesn't make six friends within three months, they don't stick. Well, teamwork evangelism dramatically increases our chances of assimilation. Plus, many people are too timid to share their faith, but they are much bolder in teams. It works."

4 Email sent to me on July 25, 2002.

5 Gibbs, *Church Next*, p. 183. When Gibbs refers to "celebration evangelism" in this quote, he's specifically referring to a new movement taking place in England. This same movement is also growing rapidly in the U.S.

## Chapter 9

1 Todd Hahn, "Leading Church for Postmoderns," *Strategies for Today's Leaders* (Summer, 2000), p. 16

2 You can see from the following list that these churches are constantly breaking records:
- Yoido Full Gospel Church (25 000 cells)
- Bethany World Prayer Center (1350 cells )
- International Charismatic Mission (14 000 cells)
- Elim Church (11 000 cells when counting children's cells)
- Christian Center of Guayaquil (1400 cells)
- Love Alive Church (1000 cells)
- Living Water Church (900 cells)
- Faith Community Baptist Church (700 cells)

3 Dale Galloway, *20-20 Vision* (Portland, OR: Scott Publishing House, 1986), p. 155.

4 I encourage pastors, however, not even to make this a goal. Many cell churches, in fact, don't even count Sunday statistics. Elim focuses on the infrastructure, though not neglecting the Sunday and weekday celebration. In 2002, an average of 116 034 attended 8500 cell groups *each week*. Elim doesn't keep statistics on how many people attend the celebration services, but after observing each of the six Sunday worship services at Elim, my estimate is upwards of 35 000 people each Sunday. It is amazing to know that three times as many people attend the cell ministry during the week as attend the celebration on Sunday! North Americans can learn important lessons from Elim. Many pastors like the idea of cells but view the "real church" as taking place on Sunday morning—and often Sunday celebration statistics are the only ones taken. Elim measures growth through the multiplication of cell groups and cell attendance. They clearly believe that the church takes place both in cells and in celebration, but the cells are the driving force of the church.

5 Some very effective cell churches are exceptions to this "norm." Crossroads UMC effectively reaches non-Christians through a seeker friendly worship service, as does Western Branch Community Church.

6 In the cell-driven strategy, people have already received their primary ministry in the cell. They are now ready to worship. It's more of a celebration of cells and the people that the cells have reached. It is not only believers who need a worship that clearly draws them to Jesus; non-Christians in a postmodern age also desire to see the living God worshipped and the true Word preached. Although people may receive Christ in the celebration gathering, the primary evangelism thrust has taken place in the cells. The people are already cared for. Sunday brings a relaxed feeling.

## Chapter 10

1 Neal F. McBride, *How to Build a Small Groups Ministry* (Colorado Springs, CO: NavPress, 1995), p. 128.

2 North Americans are accustomed to endless options. North Americans can go into a grocery store and find a dozen varieties of the same item. The cell leader training track should be exceedingly flexible.

3 My statistical study of more than 700 small-group leaders showed that small-group multiplication has nothing to do with the leader's gifts, personality, education, and so forth. It has everything to do with effort (praying for the group, visiting members, setting goals, and other characteristics that I outline in *Home Cell Group Explosion*). I believe that God desires churches to broaden their scope in this area.

## Chapter 11

1 Coaching is the key not only for cell leaders but also for pastors. Many pastors have gone to seminars and not been able to practically implement the advice they heard. A coach comes alongside the pastor to help implement that information. For pastoral coaching help, see www.cellchurchsolutions.com.

## Chapter 12

1 Eduard Schweizer, "The Service of Worship," *Neotestamentica*, Zwingli: Zurich, 1963, 335–336 as quoted in Robert and Julia Banks, *The Church Comes Home* (Sutherland, Australia: Albatross Books, 1989), p. 39.

2 First and foremost I recommend Peter Wagner's book *Discovering Your Spiritual Gift* (Ventura, CA: Regal Books, 1979). I also recommend John E. Packo's *Find and Use Your Spiritual Gifts* (Harrisburg, PA: Christian Publications, 1980) and Rick Yohn's *Discover Your Spiritual Gift* (Wheaton, IL: Tyndale House, 1982).

3 Paul's explanation of the gifts of the Spirit is in the context of the church. They are "spiritual" gifts, which are empowered by the Holy Spirit. Yet these gifts flow out of the church into the rest of life. Because most of life is spent outside the church meetings, it's important to use those gifts in all of life. A key place to exercise spiritual gifts, for example, is on the job—whether showing mercy, offering hospitality, leading a evangelistic group, practicing friendship evangelism, or praying for miracles to happen.

4 Easum, *Journal for the American Society for Church Growth*, p. 45.

## Chapter 13

1 I've shared several times throughout this book about the blessings that occur when a senior pastor is leading his own cell group and key leaders in the church are doing the same. Personal cell involvement by the lead pastor shouts to those in the congregation that the church is cell driven. The best laboratory for experimenting with and adjusting cell church principles is personal involvement. A pastor who leads a cell group captures the weekly benefits of cell ministry and can relate to fellow cell leaders in the church.

2 Cell maps and bulletin boards go a long way in making this happen. I think it's great when cell churches paste the pictures of the cell leaders on a bulletin board, highlight the latest cell retreat, and the leadership training track.

## Chapter 14

1 My original research focused on:

| Name of Church | Country | Senior Pastor | No. of Cells | Attendance |
|---|---|---|---|---|
| Bethany World Prayer Center | Baker, Louisiana | Larry Stockstill | 1100 | 8000 |
| The Christian Center of Guayaquil | Guayaquil, Ecuador | Jerry Smith | 1400 | 7000 |
| Elim Church | San Salvador, El Salvador | Mario Vega | 9000 | 35,000 |
| Faith Community Baptist Church | Singapore | Lawrence Khong | 700 | 10,000 |
| The International Charismatic Mission | Bogota, Colombia | César Castellanos | 15,000 | 45,000 |
| Love Alive Church | Tegucigalpa, Honduras | René Peñalba | 1000 | 8000 |
| Living Water Church | Lima, Perú | Juan Capuro | 1000 | 9000 |
| Yoido Full Gospel Church | Seoul, Korea | David Cho | 25,000 | 250,000 |

2 I'm teaching a doctoral course at Columbia International University on church planting—with an emphasis on cell church planting. The following books are recommended reading:

- Comiskey, Joel. *Home Cell Group Explosion.* Houston, TX: Touch Publications, 2002. 178 pp. ISBN: 1880828421.
- Garrison, David. *Church planting Movements.* Richmond, VA: International Mission Board, 2000, 60 pp. Free download at: http://www.dawnministries.org/resources/downloads/download_files/cpm_booklet.pdf
- Green, Michael, editor. *Church without Walls.* Carlisle, United Kingdom, Paternoster Press, 2002, 133 pp. ISBN: 1842271393.
- Kreider, Larry. *Helping You Build Cell Churches: A Comprehensive Training Manual for Pastors, Cell Leaders and Church Planters.* Ephrata, PA: Dove Christian Publications, 2000, 256 pp. ISBN: 1886973385.
- Shenk, David W. and Ervin R. Stutzman. *Creating Communities of the Kingdom: New Testament Models of Church Planting.* Scottsdale, PA: Herald Press, 1988, 232 pp. ISBN: 0836134702.
- Stetzer, Ed. *Planting New Churches in a Post-Modern Age* (Nashville, TN: Broadman and Holman Publishers, 2003), 365 pp. ISBN: 080542730

3 Mega cell churches are certainly preferred to mega non-cell mega churches. The mega program-based church phenomenon is growing throughout North American, but the gravest problem, in my opinion, is that such churches subtly promote anonymity. I've also noticed that a majority of the attendees are from other churches. My estimate is that seven out of ten have migrated from a smaller church to attend the mega church. Why? Often it's the freedom that comes from non-accountability. Most people involved with mega churches admit that some congregations swell their ranks with the entertaining Sunday show. Gibbs says, "It must not be assumed that the impressive growth of many seeker-sensitive churches is due primarily to the conversion of the unchurched or to the reactivatation of the once-churched-but-subsequently-lapsed. The bulk of the growth is more likely to through the transfer of church members,

either because of relocation or because of disillusionment or boredom with their former church" (Church Next, Downer's Grove, IL: InterVarsity Press, 2000, p. 173). Some who study this phenomenon compare some mega churches with a giant chain store that comes into a town and puts all the little stores out of business. The smaller churches are often drained by the mega church down the street. It has created an unhealthy celebrity focus. Celebrities have been described as people well known for their well-knowness. In contrast, those in the cell church meet together in total transparency. A cell group is the true Body of Christ, not 5000 people sitting in rows observing one man's charismatic activity. It is the basic Christian community where Christ can be transparently observed.

4  Christian Schwarz's excellent research on growing churches around the world has highlighted the fact that church planting is far more effective in actually reaching people and getting them involved in ministry than growing a mega church. He concluded that smaller churches were 1600 times more effective in winning people to Jesus that then mega churches. For more on this topic, read pp. 46–48 of *Natural Church Development* (Carol Stream, IL: ChurchSmart Resources, 1996). Large cell churches were not specifically targeted in this study, and it's my conviction that they do a far better job of seeing every member as a potential cell leader and winning souls for Jesus Christ.

5  Kreider, Larry. *Helping You Build Cell Churches: A Comprehensive Training Manual for Pastors, Cell Leaders and Church Planters*. Ephrata, PA: Dove Christian Publications, 2000, pp. 256. ISBN: 1886973385.